R
INTERNA   10   RATION

D1343609

REFERENCE

RESEARCH AND PRACTICE IN INTERNATIONAL COMMERCIAL ARBITRATION

Sources and Strategies

SI STRONG

OXFORD

UNIVERSITY PRESS

OXFORD

UNIVERSITY PRESS

Great Clarendon Street, Oxford OX2 6DP

Oxford University Press is a department of the University of Oxford.
It furthers the University's objective of excellence in research, scholarship,
and education by publishing worldwide in

Oxford New York

Auckland Cape Town Dar es Salaam Hong Kong Karachi
Kuala Lumpur Madrid Melbourne Mexico City Nairobi
New Delhi Shanghai Taipei Toronto

With offices in

Argentina Austria Brazil Chile Czech Republic France Greece
Guatemala Hungary Italy Japan Poland Portugal Singapore
South Korea Switzerland Thailand Turkey Ukraine Vietnam

Oxford is a registered trade mark of Oxford University Press
in the UK and in certain other countries

Published in the United States
by Oxford University Press Inc., New York

British Library Cataloguing in Publication Data

Data available

Library of Congress Cataloging in Publication Data

Data available

Typeset by Cepha Imaging Private Ltd, Bangalore, India
Printed by the MPG Books
Group in the UK

ISBN 978–0–19–923830–9

1 3 5 7 9 10 8 6 4 2

DEDICATION

Dedicated to my sister, Maria Strong, a fantastic attorney and a wonderful person, without whom I would not have gone into law in the first place.

—SI Strong

ACKNOWLEDGEMENTS

Every book has a beginning, and this one began with Richard M Franklin and Michael L Morkin, both brilliant international practitioners and two of the kindest lawyers I have ever met. Back in 2004, the three of us were asked to develop a regional training program in international dispute resolution for the associates in Baker & McKenzie's North American practice group. One of the first topics in the series involved research sources and strategies for international commercial arbitration, something we considered a necessary predicate to the rest of the training program and a subject of particular interest to me, given my longstanding interest in the interplay between practice and scholarship in this area of law. As I started to prepare for the training session, I discovered that there were no published materials on research methodology in international commercial arbitration, even though it is a subject that is both unique and uniquely difficult. I also realized that much of what I took for granted regarding my own research methods was actually the result of the formal and informal mentoring I received during years spent as a lawyer and solicitor in London, New York, and Chicago. The more I thought about it, the more I understood that there was more to this topic than I could share in the ninety minutes allotted to me. More needed to be said to cover the subject adequately. As it turned out, the notes I made for that training session formed the rough outline for the book that you see before you today. Therefore, I owe a great debt of gratitude to Rich, Mike, and the Baker & McKenzie North American International Dispute Resolution Training Program, for without them I never would have been inspired to write this book.

Although my name appears on the front cover, no book is ever written by one person alone, particularly when it attempts—as this one does—to draw together the diverse strands of a complex and uncodified area of legal practice. The ideas in this book are derived from the knowledge and advice that my mentors and colleagues have shared with me over the years, and I am grateful to them for their generosity in passing on their expertise. I have been incredibly fortunate in having had the chance to work with some of the best lawyers in the world and would therefore like to thank my former colleagues in the international dispute practice of Weil, Gotshal & Manges LLP, particularly Peter Gruenberger, Katherine M Oberlies, Eric Ordway, James W Quinn, Richard A Rothman, Mindy J Spector, and Kenneth L Steinthal in the New York office, as well as Michael Jones in the

London office. I would also like to express my gratitude to my former colleagues in the Chicago and London offices of Baker & McKenzie LLP. In addition to Rich and Mike, I would like to thank Thomas A Doyle, James J Dries, Michael Herington, Carmela M Hernandez, and Richard K Wagner. Furthermore, during my years in practice, I had the opportunity to act as an advocate in front of some of the world's best international arbitrators and learned much from how they handled the process. I am thankful to all of them, but most especially to Professor Dr Karl-Heinz Böckstiegel.

They say that the best way to learn a subject is to teach it, and after my experience at the University of Missouri, I could not agree more. It is a joy to teach a subject that excites you, but it is also incredibly enlightening to view the material through the eyes of a newcomer to the field. I therefore want to thank all the students who have studied International Commercial Arbitration with me at Mizzou, as well as my independent study students, since their questions and observations have done much to strengthen this book.

I also want to acknowledge my current colleagues at the University of Missouri and the Center for the Study of Dispute Resolution. They have been incredibly welcoming since I arrived here and are always willing to review draft manuscripts and discuss ideas. I am truly grateful for the scholarly community here. I also wish to acknowledge generous financial support from the University of Missouri Law School Foundation, which provided a research grant to aid in the writing of this book.

Finally, I would like to thank my colleagues and friends who have read and commented on earlier drafts of this text, including Richard M Franklin, Richard Hill, Alexis Martinez, Richard K Wagner, and Liz Williams. All errors of course remain my own.

The law is stated as it is believed to be on 1 September 2008.

Dr SI Strong

SUMMARY CONTENTS

CONTENTS

TABLE OF CASES

TABLES OF LEGISLATION, TREATIES, AND CONVENTIONS

TABLE OF CODES, RULES, AND MODEL LAWS

1

RESEARCH AND PRACTICE IN INTERNATIONAL COMMERCIAL ARBITRATION

A. Introduction

Many lawyers believe that their practice area is the most intellectually rigorous, **1.01** unique, and interesting specialty possible. From tax to real estate to commercial law to probate—it would admittedly be difficult to do well in any of these or other areas of specialization without some training. Nevertheless, those who practise in these areas of law benefit from the roots that each of these specialties has in a domestic legal system—the same legal system that the lawyers have known and prepared for since their first days of law school. However, those who venture into international commercial arbitration find themselves in deep water, indeed. Not only is it a private form of dispute resolution (which means that there are few precedents to control either outcome or procedure),[1] it requires the use of unique legal resources

---

[1] Some opponents to arbitration claim that the informality of the procedure and the lack of adherence to substantive legal principles results in a 'lawless' decision-making process. See Christopher R Drahozal, 'Is Arbitration Lawless?', 40 Loyola Law Review 187 (2006). While there may be valid concerns about certain types of domestic arbitration, many of the criticisms are not applicable to international arbitration and are, in any event, likely outweighed by the fact that arbitral awards are much easier to enforce internationally than judgments. See Philip J McConnaughay, 'The Risks and Virtues of Lawlessness: A "Second Look" at International Commercial Arbitration',

and practice methodologies. Furthermore, it is not just international—it is in ways both anational (in that it does not follow the dispute resolution procedures existing in any particular national legal system) and multinational (in that it can require the application of the laws of several different states).[2]

1.02 Although continuing legal education providers have begun to address the need for instruction in many matters regarding international commercial arbitration,[3] there is one area that is not typically discussed in those courses and seminars— research and practice methodologies.[4] While the omission is in some ways understandable—there is only so much that can be covered in a half-day or weekend seminar, particularly when attendees have mixed levels of seniority and experience in the field—it can leave newcomers to international commercial arbitration without a proper of understanding of what is required when handling these types of disputes. This is particularly dangerous when the newcomer to arbitration is very experienced in other areas of law, since the seminars do not emphasize to senior practitioners how radically research and practice in international commercial

---

93 Northwestern University Law Review 453 (1999); Linda Silberman, 'International Arbitration: Comments from a Critic', 13 American Review of International Arbitration 9 (2002).

  [2] At one point there was a movement to make international arbitration completely delocalized in the sense that it would operate outside any domestic legal system. See Julian DM Lew et al, *Comparative International Commercial Arbitration* (Kluwer Law International, 2003) para 4-49. While proponents of delocalization failed to create a process that is completely unaffected by any domestic legal system, the actual procedures used today typically do not track the rules of national civil litigation. At the same time, the transnational nature of the dispute means that there will be conflicts of legal rules and, more importantly, legal cultures. As a result, procedure in international arbitration typically represents a compromise between different national approaches.

  [3] For example, many of the major international arbitral institutions, including the International Chamber of Commerce ('ICC'), the London Court of International Arbitration ('LCIA'), and the International Centre for Dispute Resolution ('ICDR') of the American Arbitration Association ('AAA'), host continuing education courses for practitioners. Furthermore, several universities offer special certificates and/or intensive summer courses in international commercial arbitration, including: American University Washington College of Law in the United States; the School of International Arbitration at Queen Mary, University of London in the United Kingdom; the International Centre for Arbitration, Mediation and Negotiation of the Institute for European Studies of the CEU San Pablo University in Spain; and the University of Hong Kong in Hong Kong, just to name a few. Law students from around the globe can also participate in an international commercial arbitration mooting competition. See eg, Janet Walker (ed), *The Vis Book—A Participant's Guide to the Willem C Vis International Commercial Arbitration Moot* (Juris Publishing, 2008); Eric E Bergsten, 'The William C Vis International Commercial Arbitration Moot and the Teaching of International Commercial Arbitration', 22 Arbitration International 309 (2006).

  [4] There are, of course, numerous books and articles that discuss arbitral procedure at a very practical level. For example, volumes 21:4 and 23:2 of Arbitration International are devoted to advocacy and the art of arbitrating in international commercial arbitration. See also R Doak Bishop (ed), *The Art of Advocacy in International Arbitration* (Juris Publishing, 2004); United Nations Commission on International Trade Law ('UNCITRAL') Notes on Organizing Arbitral Proceedings, UN GAOR, 29th Sess, Supp No 17, UN Doc A/51/17 (1996), available at: <http://www.uncitral.org/pdf/ english/texts/arbitration/arb-notes/arb-notes-e.pdf>. However, these resources do not focus on how one goes about preparing a case to be heard in front of an international commercial arbitrator.

arbitration differ from research and practice in other areas of law. Therefore, this text focuses on research and practice strategies unique to international commercial arbitration, a topic which appears not to have been discussed in any of the literature in the field.

B. Unique Concerns Related to Research and Practice in International Commercial Arbitration

Like most legal specialties, international commercial arbitration is very much a **1.03** product of its history. For many years, practice in this area was reserved to an elite group of lawyers and law firms. Centralization made sense: international commercial arbitration required access to specialized (and expensive) resource material; utilized unique and sometimes complex procedures; involved a very small client base consisting of large international private actors; and tended to seat itself in cities that were also home to the few existing international arbitral institutions, thus limiting practitioners to those who were in geographic proximity to those institutions.

In the last ten to twenty years, however, both the economic and legal environ- **1.04** ments have changed. The easy availability of electronic databases means that non-specialists now have access to some (though not all) of the expensive specialist legal material that was once beyond their purview. Electronic mail and overnight courier systems allow lawyers to communicate quickly and efficiently with adversaries, clients, arbitrators, and arbitral institutions, regardless of location. Finally, the rapid increase in the number of private actors in the realm of international investment and commerce (due to economic globalization) has greatly expanded the international client base as well as the number of international commercial arbitrations that are filed each year.

As a result of these shifts, international commercial arbitration has become a **1.05** booming business, with increasing numbers of first-time or part-time practitioners and arbitrators. Many of these people have years of experience in litigation and/or domestic arbitration, so they are not new to the practice of law. However, international commercial arbitration is inherently different than either litigation or domestic arbitration, both in terms of the resources used in legal research, and in terms of the practices and procedures. These differences exist for three basic reasons. First, international commercial arbitration reflects a unique blend of civil and common law traditions. Experienced practitioners take this blended approach into account and do not try to mimic procedures used in domestic courts or arbitrations, lest they lose valuable opportunities to benefit their clients or, worse still, damage their credibility with the arbitrator. Second, international commercial arbitration is a private dispute resolution mechanism with few 'official' precedents or bright line rules. However, there is a wealth of persuasive authority that can help advocates make their case. Those who are new to the field may not know about these materials or how to use them, thus losing a chance to persuade the arbitrator and/or rebut (or even anticipate) an opponent's argument. Third, international commercial arbitration involves parties from different legal systems, which means that lawyers must navigate through a complex maze of jurisdictional options and potentially applicable provisions of law, all the while contending with the issues that can arise when advocates and arbitrators come from different legal cultures. Knowing the laws of one's home jurisdiction is simply not enough, even if the arbitration is seated in one's own backyard and bolstered by a choice of law provision that guarantees procedural and substantive matters will be governed by one's own national law. By its very nature, international commercial arbitration raises issues from more than one state, and lawyers must be prepared to handle those issues as they arise.

1.06 This is not to say that international commercial arbitration must remain in the hands of the same specialists who have handled such matters for decades. It does mean, however, that those who have not trained at specialist firms must be prepared for a sharp learning curve should they find themselves involved in an international commercial arbitration, no matter its size and no matter how 'domestic' it may feel at the outset.

C. Why Special Research and Practice Methodologies are Necessary in International Commercial Arbitration

1.07 Lawyers are a clever bunch. Dispute resolution specialists, in particular, are very good at picking up new information quickly and presenting a sophisticated analysis to a trier of fact and/or law. What's all the fuss about research and practice in international commercial arbitration?

1.08 The problem is when 'you don't know what you don't know'. International commercial arbitration can be misleading. At times, it can very easily look like other dispute resolution processes, particularly since there is no single, standard procedure that must be followed in all cases. This can perpetuate the notion that 'anything goes' once the process is begun. In fact, international commercial arbitration involves certain conventions that should be respected as a matter of good practice.[5] Failure to do so might not result in an unenforceable award, but could

---

[5] For example, an American lawyer who objects, courtroom style, in an arbitration will not be ejected from the hearing, but will look like a novice. Conversely, a civil law lawyer who fails to cross-examine a witness (because that procedure is foreign to civil law trials) has lost an opportunity to advance his or her case. See eg, Carmen Casado, '10 Tips for Beginning Practitioners from an

prejudice the arbitrator against one's case and/or create unnecessary conflicts with one's adversaries. Furthermore, international commercial arbitration involves certain resources and types of legal argument that might not be apparent to those who do not practise regularly in the field.

D. Benefits Associated with Learning Special Research and Practice Methodologies for International Commercial Arbitration

Legal research is typically considered the domain of junior lawyers. However, **1.09** understanding not only how to conduct legal research but how to use it is critically important in international commercial arbitration, since it is a dispute resolution process that relies heavily on written submissions. Even if more senior lawyers are not doing the hands-on tasks, they need to understand how the materials can be used if they are to present the client's case in its best light. It's particularly important for senior advocates to know how arbitrators might consider the relative weight of the different materials so that the supervising attorney can ensure that arguments are properly made, either in writing or in a hearing.

Although newcomers to the field will reap the most benefit from the principles **1.10** discussed herein, this text contains information that will be useful even to those who have acted as advocates or arbitrators in this field for many years. For example, those who have typically used traditional methods of research may be surprised at the diversity of resources available now, particularly in electronic forms. Furthermore, experienced lawyers may learn new approaches to the materials as well as new strategies regarding the presentation of one's case.

When considering the recommendations contained in the following chapters, **1.11** the reader should bear in mind that there are many ways to approach legal research and advocacy. The suggestions contained herein are but one method of proceeding. Nevertheless, the principles outlined in these pages should be useful both to those who have never considered these issues before and to those who have some practical experience in the field.

There is no need here to rehearse either the substantive or procedural principles **1.12** involved in international commercial arbitration, and indeed those subjects are far beyond the scope of this text. For those who are interested, there are several

---

ICDR Case Manager', 62 Dispute Resolution Journal 67 (Feb–Apr 2007); Alexandre de Gramont, 'In Focus: Americans find their place in the world', The National Law Journal (US) (Nov 26, 2007); Gabrielle Kaufmann-Kohler, 'Globalization of Arbitral Procedure', 36 Vanderbilt Journal of Transnational Law 1313 (2003).

excellent treatises available that discuss international arbitration from both a practical and theoretical standpoint.[6] Those who either need an overview of the field or need to research the specifics of a particular issue can look to those sources for guidance. This book is for lawyers who are ready to go beyond general treatises and general principles and conduct their own independent research.

E. How to Use This Book

1.13 This book is broken into two parts: (1) substantive chapters containing practical recommendations on research and practice in international commercial arbitration (Chapters 2–4) and (2) a bibliography of both electronic and print resources commonly used in the field (Chapter 5). Using both sections together will give readers a deep appreciation of how best to research and present a case to an international arbitrator.

1.14 The substantive chapters address three major areas of concern. Chapter 2 describes the sources available in international commercial arbitration and how they are used. International commercial arbitration is a private dispute resolution process that blends civil and common law traditions while simultaneously utilizing elements of both an anational and a multinational approach. As a result, the resources in this field are fundamentally different than the legal resources used in domestic dispute resolution. Those who wish to be an effective advocate or arbitrator in this area of law must therefore learn: (1) what legal authorities exist in international arbitration; (2) how experienced advocates use those authorities; and (3) what weight experienced arbitrators give those authorities. These three topics form the basis of Chapter 2.

1.15 It is not just that the materials in international commercial arbitration are different than those used in other forms of dispute resolution; the materials are also difficult to find.[7] Chapter 3 discusses: (1) where to locate the materials unique to international commercial arbitration as well as (2) how those materials are typically used in researching common areas of dispute, including: arbitration agreements; arbitral procedure; challenges to an arbitrator; and recognition, enforcement,

---

[6] Four of the best are Gary B Born, *International Commercial Arbitration* (Kluwer Law International, 2008); Emmanuel Gaillard and John Savage (eds), *Fouchard, Gaillard, Goldman on International Commercial Arbitration* (Kluwer Law International, 1999); Julian DM Lew et al, *Comparative International Commercial Arbitration* (Kluwer Law International, 2003); and Alan Redfern and Martin Hunter et al, *Law and Practice of International Commercial Arbitration* (Sweet & Maxwell, 2004). For specialized commentary regarding arbitration at the International Chamber of Commerce, see Yves Derains and Eric A Schwartz, *A Guide to the ICC Rules of Arbitration* (Kluwer Law International, 2005).

[7] See eg, Dr Emmanuel Jolivet, 'Access to Information and Awards', 22 Arbitration International 265 (2006).

and challenge of an award. However, one does not necessarily use the same research materials to address each of these subjects. For example, research on enforcement of an award will focus on conventions, treaties, domestic legislation, and case law, since enforcement issues fall naturally within the exclusive province of the courts (though the researcher will have to deal with the question of which court). Using the same research techniques to investigate arbitral procedure would lead to disaster, since procedural issues are very much committed to the arbitrator's discretion. Thus, lawyers investigating procedural concerns would focus much more heavily on reported arbitral awards, arbitral rules, treatises, and other learned works. However, since procedural errors can result in enforcement problems,[8] one would be well advised to consult—but not rely entirely upon— domestic law as well.

The issue of how to apply one's research continues in Chapter 4, which discusses   **1.16**
the practical aspects of legal research. For example, an American advocate might
be inclined to string together several citations to American cases in support of a
particular legal proposition. Although this technique would be well received in a
domestic litigation or arbitration, it would not be looked upon as favourably in
an international arbitration. Similarly, an advocate trained in the civil law tradition might rely heavily on treatises and/or statutes to support his or her argument, even when a common law lawyer is acting adversely or as the arbitrator.
Failing to give due weight to judicial decisions in those circumstances could lead
to disaster. This chapter thus helps advocates and arbitrators realize how different
legal materials can and should be used in an international arbitral proceeding.
The chapter also covers issues such as how to adapt pleadings to take into account
the legal traditions of one's arbitrators or adversaries; how to present one's research
formally (including citation forms) and procedurally; and how to submit written
testimony from expert witnesses.

Chapter 5 consists of a bibliography supplemented by additional instruction on   **1.17**
how to find and use each of the materials. The bibliography also recognizes the
realities of the electronic age and includes references not only to possible print
locations but also to electronic locations.

With these guidelines in place, it is time to discuss the many possible sources of   **1.18**
law in the field of international commercial arbitration.

---

[8] See eg, Convention on the Recognition and Enforcement of Foreign Arbitral Awards, art V,
June 10, 1958, 330 UNTS 3 ('New York Convention').

2

SOURCES OF LAW IN INTERNATIONAL COMMERCIAL ARBITRATION

A. Introduction

From the earliest days of their careers, lawyers are trained to recognize the appro-   **2.01**
priate sources of legal authority in their home jurisdictions. For common law
lawyers, statutes and judicial opinions form the fundamental sources of law, with
the relative weight of each varying according to national constitutional principles.
For example, the United Kingdom follows the principle of Parliamentary sover-
eignty, which means that the courts ultimately defer to the legislature. The United
States takes the opposite view. Not only do judges play a significant role in interpreting statutes, but courts are empowered to strike down federal or state legislation that violates fundamental principles of constitutional law. Furthermore,
case law makes up the bulk of certain areas of substantive law—such as tort or
contract—in many common law jurisdictions. Naturally, whenever an advocate
is researching substantive law, he or she can and should use whatever research
methodologies would be appropriate in a litigation involving the same national
laws and legal issues.

2.02 Lawyers from civil law jurisdictions view legal authority quite differently. Although judicial decisions carry some weight, jurists from the civil law tradition focus much more heavily on the text of the relevant code provisions and on the opinions of esteemed legal commentators when deciding disputes. To the extent case law exists in these jurisdictions, it typically reflects judicial interpretation of statutory law, and does not—as in common law systems—constitute the core of the substantive law. It stands to reason, then, that an advocate or arbitrator from a civil law jurisdiction will not place the same value on a judicial opinion that a common law lawyer will. Similarly, a common law lawyer may not think to introduce legal commentary if judicial precedent weighs heavily in the common law lawyer's favour, even though an arbitrator from a civil law tradition might find the commentator's opinion more persuasive than court decisions.[1]

2.03 Traditionally, international commercial arbitration has incorporated elements of both common law and civil law traditions into its procedures, and the same duality exists in the types of authorities that arbitrators find persuasive. Furthermore, international commercial arbitration is, by definition, international, and thus requires advocates and arbitrators to understand the interplay between national and international law.

2.04 As if considering civil law traditions, common law traditions, and international complexities weren't enough, lawyers involved in international commercial arbitration also have to contend with the fact that there are some types of legal authorities that are unique to this field of law. It is not enough to research the law as it stands in the relevant jurisdiction(s); to prepare properly, advocates must also seek out materials from specialized arbitral reporters. Failure to do so can seriously prejudice a client's case.

2.05 Even this very brief overview demonstrates how complicated research and practice can be in this field. Being a good lawyer in one's home jurisdiction is not enough. Those who wish to be an effective advocate or arbitrator in international commercial arbitration must know: (1) what legal authorities exist in international arbitration; (2) how experienced advocates use those authorities; and (3) what weight experienced arbitrators give those authorities. These subjects are covered in this chapter.

---

[1] Although civil law lawyers do not rely heavily on judicial precedent as a general rule, international commercial arbitration is one area where an exception may be made, at least among French courts and practitioners. See Emmanuel Gaillard and John Savage (eds), *Fouchard, Gaillard, Goldman on International Commercial Arbitration* (Kluwer Law International, 1999) (stating 'French international arbitration law is thus currently drawn from two sources: a brief, liberal Code of Civil Procedure, and well-established case law that is generally able to overcome the Code's shortcomings . . . and to deal with difficulties of interpretation which may yet arise').

B. Legal Authorities in International Commercial Arbitration

Every advocate and arbitrator comes into an international arbitration with a **2.06** vast amount of expertise, all of which is valuable. The expertise may relate to the factual or legal elements of the dispute or to the national law that is anticipated to control the merits or procedure of the matter. However, a high degree of competence in these areas does not guarantee an equal amount of knowledge as to how international arbitrations are and should be conducted. This is not to say that lawyers who have achieved a great deal of success in domestic dispute resolution cannot do well in international arbitration. However, those who do not specialize in international arbitration have to supplement their domestic expertise if they want to compete at the highest level.

The first thing that a non-specialist needs to understand about international **2.07** commercial arbitration is the variety of legal authorities that are available. Some of these authorities contain mandatory provisions of law and others contain principles that are merely persuasive. The situation is further complicated by the fact that some authorities that would be either binding or persuasive in a domestic dispute do not necessarily have the same weight in an international dispute.

There are eight different types of authority in international commercial arbitration, **2.08** though not all of them apply to every dispute that may arise during a proceeding. Notably, the separation of legal authority into eight separate categories does not take into account the fact that there may at times be conflicts over which nation's law controls any particular issue. Quite often, the national law of one country governs one aspect of the dispute while the national law of another country governs another aspect. While this split of authority most often reflects the procedural-substantive divide, where one nation's law governs procedural matters (the term 'governs' is used advisedly in this context, since, as will be discussed later, arbitral procedure does not imitate judicial procedure) and another nation's law governs substantive issues, it is entirely possible to have a situation where the law of two different nations governs either procedural issues[2] or substantive issues.[3] Furthermore, there are instances where supranational (such as European) law may need to be considered.[4] Even more confusingly, the law of yet another nation may become relevant when it comes time to enforce the award.[5]

---

[2] See eg, *Union of India v McDonnell Douglas Corporation* [1993] 2 Lloyd's Law Rep 48.
[3] See eg, *Buyer (Mozambique) v Seller (The Netherlands)*, XIII Yearbook Commercial Arbitration 110 (1988).
[4] See eg, *Eco Swiss China Time Ltd v Benetton Int'l NV*, 1 June 1999, Case C-126/97, [1999] ECR I-3055.
[5] See eg, Convention on the Recognition and Enforcement of Foreign Arbitral Awards, art V(2)(b), June 10, 1958, 330 UNTS 3 ('New York Convention').

2.09   The eight categories of legal authority in international commercial arbitration are:

- conventions and treaties;
- national laws;
- arbitral rules;
- law of the dispute (procedural orders and agreements between the parties);
- arbitral awards;
- case law;
- treatises and monographs; and
- legal articles.

2.10   The following sections discuss each type of authority in turn. However, some background information on international commercial law may be useful to help non-specialists understand how state law relates to what can be termed truly private law—the law 'created' by and between the parties.

(1) Sources of law—state sources versus private sources

2.11   Part of the difficulty that non-specialists have with international commercial arbitration relates to the fact that authorities in this field can be generated by both public sources (states) and private sources (ranging from international arbitral institutions to the parties themselves). The mere fact that a dispute can be controlled by multiple sources of law is not, of itself, problematic. For example, lawyers who specialize in litigation, either in the national or international context, are used to dealing with a wide variety of relevant sources of law, ranging from domestic statutes and case law to international treaties and conventions. All of these materials are easily found and used by advocates. To the extent an unfamiliar issue arises—even one of international law—the lawyer is equipped to handle it, since questions of law are always interpreted through the lens of the national legal system in which the lawyer habitually operates.

2.12   Furthermore, some lawyers—those that handle domestic arbitration, for instance—are familiar with so-called private sources of law. Unlike pure litigators, advocates in domestic arbitration understand the interplay between state-generated sources of authority (such as statutes and judicial opinions) and party- or arbitrator-generated sources of authority (such as arbitration agreements, arbitral rules, and procedural orders). However, experts in domestic arbitration need to exercise caution, since some of the legal or procedural norms that apply in a domestic arbitration do not apply equally to international arbitrations. International commercial arbitration is, in many ways, as different from domestic arbitration as it is from national or even international litigation.

2.13   Those who are entering the realm of international commercial arbitration for the first time are likely to hear the phrase 'private form of justice' and may think that it refers to the fact that a private individual or panel of individuals hears the dispute in a confidential (non-public) proceeding rather than have the dispute publicly heard in a courtroom by a judge and/or jury. While this is certainly true, the term goes far deeper than that. Parties in international commercial arbitration have enormous latitude in shaping the governing procedures, subject only to certain provisions of mandatory law being imposed by states with a sufficiently close legal nexus to the resolution of the dispute.[6] The parties' governing choices are typically found in the arbitration agreement and/or the substantive contract, but are also reflected in any arbitral rules or guidelines that have been incorporated into the procedure, either through the arbitration agreement itself or through a procedural order handed down by the arbitrator.

Treatises on international arbitration also make much of the discretion given to the arbitrator, and rightfully so.[7] At times, it can seem as if it is the arbitrator who controls the procedure, not the parties. However, although most arbitral rules give arbitrators a great deal of discretion to decide how to proceed[8] (an approach which is also approved in many national statutes and judicial opinions),[9] that discretion is bounded on two sides. On the one hand, arbitrators may not violate mandatory provisions of relevant state law. On the other hand, arbitrators may not disregard explicit joint instructions from the parties (again, so long as the instructions do not violate mandatory provisions of state law). Therefore, arbitrator discretion—though potentially broad—is not unlimited.

2.14

---

[6] The issue of which state laws control certain issues and which state courts have the ability to intervene in an arbitration is beyond the scope of this text. However, there are several excellent treatises that address this subject. See generally Gary B Born, *International Commercial Arbitration* (Kluwer Law International, 2008); Emmanuel Gaillard and John Savage (eds), *Fouchard, Gaillard, Goldman on International Commercial Arbitration* (Kluwer Law International, 1999); Julian DM Lew et al, *Comparative International Commercial Arbitration* (Kluwer Law International, 2003); and Alan Redfern and Martin Hunter et al, *Law and Practice of International Commercial Arbitration* (Sweet & Maxwell, 2004). For specialized commentary regarding arbitration at the International Chamber of Commerce, see Yves Derains and Eric A Schwartz, *A Guide to the ICC Rules of Arbitration* (Kluwer Law International, 2005).

[7] See eg, Redfern and Hunter et al (n 6), para 6-02.

[8] See eg, American Arbitration Association International Rules ('AAA International Rules'), art 16; China International Economic and Trade Arbitration Commission ('CIETAC Rules'), art 29; Rules of Arbitration of the International Chamber of Commerce ('ICC Rules'), arts 15, 17; Arbitration Rules of the London Court of International Arbitration ('LCIA Rules'), art 14; Swiss Rules of International Arbitration ('Swiss Rules'), art 15; United Nations Commission on International Trade Law Arbitration Rules ('UNCITRAL Rules'), art 15.

[9] See eg, English Arbitration Act 1996, s 34; French Code of Civil Procedure, book IV, art 1494; Swiss Private International Law Act of 1987, art 182; United Nations Commission on International Trade Law Model Law on International Commercial Arbitration of 2006 ('UNCITRAL Model Law'), art 19; *Bremer Vulkan Schiffbau und Maschinenfabrik Respondents v South India Shipping Corp Ltd* [1981] AC 909 (English law); *Karaha Bodas Co, LLC v Perusahaan Pertambangan Minyak Dan Gas Bumi Negara*, 364 F3d 274 (5th Cir 2004) (US law); *Al-Haddad Commodities Corp v Toepfer Intern Asia Pte, Ltd*, 485 F Supp 2d 677 (ED Va 2007) (US law).

2.15 The process is not completely in the hands of the arbitrators and the parties, however. States retain firm control over certain aspects of the process. For example, parties cannot violate due process and public policy, no matter what they may agree among themselves. Similarly, a state may legitimately decide that certain areas of substantive law are non-arbitrable.[10] However, the fact that a state retains residual control over certain aspects of the process does not mean that arbitration needs to follow the procedural rules laid down by the national courts of any particular state. So long as the arbitral procedure complies with certain basic principles of law, such as international due process and international public policy,[11] the process can look as similar or dissimilar to a litigation as the parties and arbitrator wish. Indeed, one of the great benefits of arbitration is its ability to tailor the procedure to best suit the dispute.[12] Lawyers who insist on the same type and degree of formality as exists in domestic or even international litigation not only look like novices, they rob themselves of one of the advantages of this form of dispute resolution.

2.16 With this in mind, we turn to each of the eight forms of legal authority in international commercial arbitration.

(2) Sources of law—international conventions and treaties

2.17 One of the primary reasons why private commercial actors choose to arbitrate transnational disputes rather than litigate them is because arbitral awards are much easier to enforce internationally than are judgments. The difference in enforceability rates is due to several multinational conventions for the enforcement of arbitral awards, the foremost of which is the United Nations' 1958 Convention on the Recognition and Enforcement of Foreign Arbitral Awards ('New York Convention').[13] Although the New York Convention, with 142 state signatories, is one of the most successful international agreements to date, other regional and multinational conventions also promote the easy international enforcement of arbitral awards.[14]

2.18 Although the content of every convention is different, most include the requirements for enforcing a foreign arbitral award. For example, a party who wishes to enforce an award may need to have the original or a certified copy of the award

---

[10] For example, intellectual property matters are non-arbitrable in the European Union.

[11] See generally New York Convention (n 5), art V.

[12] Born (n 6), at 7–9; W Mark C Weidemaier, 'Arbitration and the Individuation Critique', 49 Arizona Law Review 69 (2007).

[13] New York Convention (n 5).

[14] See eg, European Convention on International Commercial Arbitration, Apr 21, 1961, 484 UNTS 364 ('Geneva Convention'); Inter-American Convention on International Commercial Arbitration of 1976, Jan 30, 1975, 1438 UNTS 245, 14 ILM 336 ('Panama Convention').

and the arbitration agreement in hand as well as a certified translation.[15] The convention may also set forth limited grounds for objections to enforcement and allow the signatory state to make certain reservations regarding the types of arbitrations that will be subject to the terms of the convention.[16]

Many advocates and arbitrators do not focus on enforcement issues until after the conclusion of an arbitration. That is a mistake. Everyone involved in the process must keep in mind from the earliest stage of the process that a future award may need to be enforced under the terms of one of these conventions. Therefore, both advocates and arbitrators should review the terms of any relevant convention(s) or enforcement mechanisms well before enforcement becomes an issue so as to be sure that the arbitral procedure complies with the necessary requirements from the very beginning. **2.19**

Enforcement issues are typically not something that lawyers versed in domestic arbitration have to think about, but it is of critical importance in international arbitration, lest the parties find—after extensive and expensive proceedings—that the award has been nullified due to some sort of error early on. Lawyers who are experienced in national or international litigation also run the risk of over-looking the importance of matters relating to enforcement. Thus, those who are new to international commercial arbitration have to train themselves to consider enforcement issues from the very beginning of the process. **2.20**

Enforcement agreements are not the only types of international instruments that are important in this area of practice.[17] Other relevant international agreements not only address enforcement issues but also include procedural guidelines for the resolution of disputes.[18] One of the most important instruments describing both enforcement and procedural requirements is the Convention on the Settlement of Investment Disputes between States and Nationals of Other States ('ICSID Convention' or 'Washington Convention').[19] **2.21**

Although treaties involving the arbitration of investment disputes are by far the most numerous of these types of international agreements (ie, including provisions regarding both procedure and enforcement), there are other similar instruments. Perhaps the most well-known example is the Iran-United States Claims Tribunal, which resolves commercial claims relating to the breakdown in US-Iranian **2.22**

---

[15] See eg, New York Convention (n 5), art IV.

[16] Ibid, arts I, V.

[17] The nomenclature of these instruments—which can include 'convention', 'treaty', or 'agreement'—is not indicative of the content and scope of the agreement.

[18] Many of these treaties involve international investment and can be multilateral or bilateral in nature.

[19] Convention on the Settlement of Investment Disputes between States and Nationals of Other States, Mar 18, 1965, 575 UNTS 159 ('ICSID Convention').

relations following the Iranian Revolution in 1979.[20] There are not a large number of such special-purpose arbitration treaties and agreements, but practitioners need to be aware of them so that they don't misfile a claim.[21]

2.23 There are two important international instruments that cannot be called either a treaty or a convention. Both are promulgated by the United Nations Commission on International Trade Law ('UNCITRAL'). The first is known as the UNCITRAL Arbitration Rules and will be discussed below in the section on arbitral rules. The second is known as the UNCITRAL Model Law on International Commercial Arbitration and will be discussed in the section immediately following, which concerns national laws.

(3) Sources of law—national laws

2.24 When non-specialists think about what constitutes a relevant legal authority, national law is usually what first comes to mind. Most states have some sort of statute governing arbitration as well as judicial opinions discussing the application of the relevant legislation. However, those who are new to this area of practice need to understand that not all of the provisions of a domestically applicable statute or judicial opinion will necessarily apply to an international dispute.[22] Furthermore, some states enact different provisions that apply only to international arbitrations.[23] In addition, federalized states may involve several layers of legislation.[24]

---

[20] See Declaration of the Government of the Democratic and Popular Republic of Algeria Concerning the Settlement of Claims by the Government of the United States of America and the Government of the Islamic Republic of Iran Jan 19, 1981, 20 ILM 230 ('Algiers Declaration').

[21] For example, arbitrators have been involved in assisting the Claims Resolution Tribunal for Dormant Accounts in Switzerland, see <http://www.crt-ii.org/_crt-i/frame.html>, and the International Commission on Holocaust Era Insurance Claims, see <http://www.icheic.org>.

[22] For example, US domestic awards may be set aside on the grounds of 'manifest disregard of law' even though many internationalists hold that manifest disregard is an improper ground for non-enforcement of a foreign arbitral award under the New York Convention. See eg, Hans Smit, 'Is Manifest Disregard of the Law or the Evidence or Both a Ground for Vacatur of an Arbitral Award?', 8 American Review of International Arbitration 341 (1997).

[23] For example, the first chapter of the US Federal Arbitration Act ('FAA') covers domestic US arbitration. See 9 USC §§ 1–16. International arbitrations governed by the New York Convention are covered in chapter two of the FAA, see ibid §§ 201–8, while international arbitrations governed by the Panama Convention are covered in chapter three, see ibid §§ 301–7. Chapter one only applies to matters brought under chapters two and three to the extent that it is not inconsistent with the provisions of the later chapters. See ibid §§ 208, 307. Other states structure their legislation differently. For example, in England, Part I of the Arbitration Act 1996 applies to all arbitrations, although 'domestic arbitrations' are also subject to certain provisions of Part II; furthermore, special provisions for recognizing and enforcing certain foreign arbitral awards are contained in Part III of the Arbitration Act 1996.

[24] For example, there is some debate in the United States about the extent to which state law provisions supplement the international aspects of the Federal Arbitration Act. Born (n 6), at 341–57. Switzerland handles the matter somewhat differently, explicitly providing that the national legislation

For the most part, national statutes governing international arbitration do not **2.25** outline the precise steps that parties must follow during the arbitration itself. Instead, the statutes typically focus on defining the relationship between the national courts and the arbitral proceedings. For example, a statute might indicate what assistance a court can provide to an arbitrator and at what point in the proceedings. Courts may be given the right to involve themselves in the dispute in the period of time before the arbitration has properly begun, particularly if parties need interim relief to protect property or rights or if the claimant needs to compel a recalcitrant defendant to enter into arbitration. National courts also have the right to become involved at the end of the dispute, when parties seek to enforce or set aside an award. The more difficult question is the extent to which a court can or should become involved while the arbitration is in progress. Some state statutes—such as those in effect in France—take the position that a court may not intervene in a dispute once the arbitrator has accepted jurisdiction over the matter.[25] Other states give their courts some power to act during this intermediate period, although that power may only be invoked upon the request of the arbitrator.[26] In any situation where a party wishes to invoke the power of a state court, the national law on arbitration is the place to begin the inquiry.

Another area that is typically covered by national laws involves the question of **2.26** whether the dispute is one which can be resolved through arbitration. There are typically two separate concepts at work here. The first is *compétence-compétence* (also known as *Kompetenz-Kompetenz*), which addresses the issue of whether an arbitrator is competent to decide his or her own jurisdiction. Some states allow the arbitrator to make such preliminary decisions, although the state retains the ability to nullify the award after the arbitration has concluded if it turns out that the arbitrator did not act within the scope of the powers granted by arbitration agreement. Other states take the position that early court review of jurisdictional questions is better as a matter of public policy and thus allow parties to seek a ruling on jurisdiction even after the arbitration has begun. In either case, the parties look to national law—embodied in statutes and/or case law—to determine whether and to what extent they may bring an action in court to determine the arbitrator's competence to decide his or her own jurisdiction.

The second concept that addresses the question of whether a dispute may be **2.27** resolved through arbitration involves arbitrability. Here, the idea is that the state may reserve certain disputes to its own national courts as a matter of public policy.

---

will apply unless the parties have agreed that it shall not or that cantonal law on arbitration shall apply. Swiss Private International Law of 1987, art 176.

[25] French Code of Civil Procedure, book IV, art 1458.

[26] See eg, English Arbitration Act 1996, ss 42–5; Swiss Private International Law of 1987, art 183; United States Federal Arbitration Act, § 7.

For example, in the European Union, matters involving intellectual property must be resolved through public dispute resolution mechanisms, not private ones.[27] At one point, anti-trust or competition law matters were thought to be reserved to national courts, though that view has changed in recent years.[28] This is one area where lawyers may need to look beyond the relevant arbitration statute, since state determinations about arbitrability may not be discussed in those provisions but instead may be reflected in statutes governing substantive provisions of law or in judicial opinions.

2.28　Issues involving arbitrability and *compétence-compétence* illustrate two types of mandatory provisions of law. Despite the high degree of respect given to party autonomy in international commercial arbitration, participants typically cannot contract around these sorts of mandatory principles. States may also have other provisions of mandatory law that parties to an arbitration must consider. For example, many states indicate that certain basic principles of due process or public policy are non-derogable.[29] Although commentators argue that issues involving due process and public policy in an international arbitration are governed by international, as opposed to domestic, standards, some state courts defy that view and apply the standards reflected in their own national laws.[30] Parties need to be aware of any mandatory provisions of relevant state law, lest the final award be unenforceable.

2.29　One area of national law that many non-specialists believe applies to international arbitration involves the rules governing civil procedure in national courts. That is not the case. As discussed below, arbitral procedure is decided by the arbitrator, subject to the agreement of the parties and any applicable arbitral rules. Domestic civil procedure is not a mandatory provision of law that must be followed in an international arbitration. Furthermore, as a matter of good practice, neither the parties nor the arbitrator should choose to be bound by the procedures used in national courts, since to do so would defeat the informality and flexibility, and possibly also the neutrality, that are the hallmarks of arbitration. Nevertheless, lawyers who are unfamiliar with international commercial arbitration may try to resort to the procedures that are most familiar to them,

---

[27] Lew (n 6), para 9-64.

[28] See eg, *Eco Swiss China Time Ltd v Benetton International NV*, Case C-126/97 (1999) XXIV Yearbook Commercial Arbitration 629; *Mitsubishi Motors Corp v Soler Chrysler Plymouth Inc*, 473 US 614 (1985).

[29] Most international conventions on enforcement support this position, recognizing that an objection to enforcement can be lodged based on either principle. See eg, New York Convention (n 5), art V.

[30] See eg, *Seller (Russian Federation) v Buyer (Germany)*, CLOUT Case 402: Bayerisches Oberstes Landesgericht, XXVII Yearbook Commercial Arbitration 445 (2002) and 263 (2002); *Jiangsu Changlong Chem Co, Inc v Burlington Bio-Med & Sci Corp*, 399 F Supp 2d 165, 168 (EDNY 2005) (US).

ie, those that are used in domestic litigation, either: (a) because the lawyers do not realize that what they consider to be default or universal rules of procedure are not, in fact, used in other jurisdictions and/or in arbitration, or (b) because the lawyers believe that the procedural rules used in domestic litigation will benefit their client more than the arbitral rules will.[31] Although attorneys may argue—as a tactical matter—that certain rules of civil procedure should apply by analogy to a particular arbitration, they should make it clear that they know that rules of civil procedure are not applicable as a matter of right. Failure to acknowledge the differences in arbitral and judicial procedure can damage lawyers' credibility and/or alienate the arbitrator. Furthermore, inexperienced counsel can waste a great deal of time and money by arguing that domestic rules of court should be applied in an international arbitration. Therefore, reference to domestic civil procedures should be made sparingly and with great caution.

When considering questions of national law in an international arbitral proceed- **2.30** ing, advocates and arbitrators often must determine which national law applies to: (a) the substance and (b) the procedure of the dispute. The relevant substantive law is usually relatively easy to ascertain, since sophisticated parties typically include a choice of law provision in the contract at issue. There may some debate about whether the laws of any other states also apply, either because certain non-contractual claims have been deemed to fall within the scope of the arbitration agreement and/or because certain mandatory provisions of law may apply despite the parties' attempt to contract out of those provisions. In spite of these sorts of complexities, the analysis of the substantive choice of law typically follows well-known conflict of law principles used in international litigation.[32]

However, there are several issues involving substantive law that can surprise **2.31** newcomers to international commercial arbitration. First, over the course of time, international commerce has recognized a body of legal principles known as *lex mercatoria*, also known as the international law merchant. International contracts will occasionally choose this body of law to govern commercial relationships or, in some cases, an arbitrator may choose to apply the *lex mercatoria* if no other law has been chosen by the parties. Though a full discussion of

---

[31] For example, a US-trained lawyer might believe that the type of far-reaching discovery that is available in US courts—including both extensive document discovery and oral depositions in advance of any hearing—is necessary or useful in proving his or her case in arbitration. However, discovery—both oral and written—is not available as a matter of right in most international arbitrations, and any party disclosure ordered by the arbitrator is likely to be much narrower than a US-trained lawyer will be able to obtain in a domestic American litigation.

[32] A discussion of these principles is beyond the scope of this book, but helpful material may be found in texts such as Lawrence Collins et al, *Dicey, Collins & Morris on the Conflict of Laws* (Sweet & Maxwell, 2008) and Eckart Gottschalk et al, *Conflict of Laws in a Globalized World* (Cambridge University Press, 2007).

lex mercatoria is beyond the scope of this text, the concept has been known and discussed in its modern form for decades.[33]

2.32 Second, parties to arbitration can incorporate the United Nations Convention on the International Sale of Goods ('CISG'),[34] either through an express choice or, in the absence of an express provision, through reference to the national law of a signatory state. The CISG has been ratified by seventy-one countries and offers its own set of substantive legal rules on which contracting parties, courts, and arbitrators may rely. Adoption of the CISG may be particularly common in arbitrations involving Middle Eastern or Arab nations.

2.33 Third, parties can incorporate basic notions of international law, including the general principles of civilized states, as contemplated by article 38 of the Statute of the International Court of Justice.[35] Again, recourse to these concepts may be particularly common in arbitrations involving Arab or Middle Eastern parties, since doing so will minimize problems associated with the selection of a national law that incorporates principles of Shariah law. It is likely that issues involving commercial application of Shariah law will become increasingly urgent in coming years.

2.34 Determining the relevant procedural law can be a more difficult issue for those who are new to this field. First, in international arbitration, the term 'procedural law' does not mean the types of detailed rules of civil procedure applicable to a domestic litigation. Instead, the term refers to the backdrop of procedural rules regarding access to courts during an arbitration as well as mandatory principles of procedural law, such as due process. Courts located where the arbitration is seated are considered competent to address procedural issues arising out of the arbitration, and those courts typically apply their own national laws to any disputes before them. Thus, the national law of the place where the arbitration is seated (the *lex arbitri*) is always relevant to procedural questions. As a matter of theory, however, parties can choose to have the procedural law of another state apply to the proceedings. The full extent to which the parties can oust the application of the procedural law of the arbitral seat is unclear, but it appears unlikely that the parties can contract entirely out of the procedural law of the seat.[36] Since any attempt to do so would likely result in expensive and time consuming litigation and/or arbitration, parties are encouraged to be cautious when attempting

---

[33] See eg, Klaus Peter Berger, *The Creeping Codification of Lex Mercatoria* (Kluwer Law International, 1993); Thomas E Carbonneau (ed), *Lex Mercatoria and Arbitration: A Discussion of the New Law Merchant* (JurisNet, LLC, 1998); Lord Justice Mustill, 'The New *Lex Mercatoria*: The First Twenty-Five Years', 4 Arbitration International 86 (1988).

[34] UN Doc A/CONF.97/18 (1980), reprinted in 19 ILM 671 (1980).

[35] June 26, 1945, 156 UNTS 77.

[36] See eg, *Union of India v McDonnell Douglas Corporation* [1993] 2 Lloyd's Law Rep 48.

to invoke the procedural law of any state other than the law of the seat of the arbitration.

There is at least one circumstance in which the procedural law of a state other **2.35** than the arbitral seat may become relevant. Certain international conventions, including the New York Convention, indicate that a court may apply its own public policies when considering whether to permit an objection to enforcement of a foreign arbitral award.[37] Furthermore, some states have considered some principles of procedural due process so important that they raise them to the level of public policy, thus allowing domestic procedural rules of a state other than the seat of arbitration to affect the enforceability of an award.[38] While this sort of practice is obviously problematic, it still occurs from time to time.

Because every nation has its own view of arbitration, the content of different **2.36** national laws on arbitration can vary widely. However, as international commercial arbitration has become more common, there has been a push to standardize national provisions and encourage a pro-arbitration stance around the world. The most important harmonizing mechanism is the UNCITRAL Model Law on International Commercial Arbitration,[39] which has been in existence for over twenty years and which has been adopted in whole or in part by over fifty-five nation states or autonomous regions. By adopting the UNCITRAL Model Law, nations indicate their acceptance of certain basic principles of arbitration law and make it more likely that foreign parties will conduct business with entities based in the adopting state, since the foreign parties can anticipate how national courts will handle issues involving international commercial arbitration. Although the mere adoption of the UNCITRAL Model Law does not mean that national courts in one state will apply or interpret particular provisions in the same way as national courts in other states that have adopted the UNCITRAL Model Law, it does provide a useful starting point for analysis. Ultimately, however, parties must remember that the UNCITRAL Model Law is just that—a model—that may be interpreted and applied differently in every jurisdiction into which it is brought.

In the area of substantive law, *lex mercatoria* appears as a legal principle that might **2.37** be unfamiliar to those who have not practised extensively in international commercial arbitration. There are also two procedural principles that can surprise newcomers to the field. Traditionally, parties have been permitted to grant an

---

[37] New York Convention (n 5), art V(2)(b).

[38] See eg, *Seller (Russian Federation) v Buyer (Germany)*, CLOUT Case 402: Bayerisches Oberstes Landesgericht, XXVII Yearbook Commercial Arbitration 445 (2002) and 263 (2002); SI Strong, 'Enforcing Class Arbitration in the International Sphere: Due Process and Public Policy Concerns', 30 University of Pennsylvania Journal of International Law 1, 59–60 (2008).

[39] GA Res 40/72, 40 UN GAOR Supp (No 17), UN Doc A/40/17 (June 21, 1985), also available at <http://www.uncitral.org/uncitral/en/uncitral_texts/arbitration/1985Model_arbitration.html>.

arbitrator the power to decide a dispute *ex aqueo et bono* or as an *amiable compositeur*. Though the two powers are slightly different, both involve the application of equitable principles to the decision-making process rather than the strict adherence to legal principles.[40] Arbitrators do not exercise these powers unless given express authorization to do so by the parties, so parties should not worry that international arbitrators will render a 'lawless' award based on nothing but vague equitable principles on their own accord. Some arbitral rules also provide an express presumption against application of equitable principles.[41] However, parties can find it useful to grant these powers to an arbitrator.

(4) Sources of law—arbitral rules

2.38 Most newcomers to international commercial arbitration are surprised to learn about the variety of 'private' sources of law. One of the most important of the private sources are procedural rules promulgated by national and international arbitration institutions. Typically, arbitral institutions carry out two distinct duties: (1) the promulgation of a detailed set of rules governing arbitral procedure (similar, but not identical to rules of civil procedure used in national courts) and (2) the administration of arbitrations (which may include tasks such as naming and hearing challenges to arbitrators, facilitating communication between the parties, holding the official file, and reviewing the arbitral award for procedural accuracy). Leading international arbitral institutions include the International Chamber of Commerce ('ICC'), the London Court of International Arbitration ('LCIA'), the International Centre for Dispute Resolution ('ICDR') based out of the American Arbitration Association ('AAA'), the Arbitration Institute of the Stockholm Chamber of Commerce ('SCC') and the Singapore International Arbitration Centre ('SIAC'), just to name a few.[42] Though each of these rule sets gives a great deal of discretion to the arbitrator, they provide some structure to arbitral proceedings by addressing issues such as how arbitrators can be named and challenged, how the arbitration is to be commenced, procedural timetables, some guidance regarding the presentation of evidence (for example, whether hearings or written witness statements are required or permitted), the making of the award, etc. In most instances, the rules constitute default scenarios that can be amended or disregarded through party agreement.

---

[40] See eg, Leon Trakman, '*Ex Aqueo et Bono*: Demystifying an Ancient Concept', 8 Chicago Journal of International Law 621 (2008).

[41] See eg, American Arbitration Association International Rules, art 28; Rules of Arbitration of the International Chamber of Commerce, art 17; Arbitration Rules of the London Court of International Arbitration, arts 22.3 and 22.4.

[42] For more on the differences between individual rule sets, see Simpson, Thacher & Bartlett LLP, *Comparison of International Arbitration Rules* (Juris Publishing, 2002); Hans Smit, *A Chart Comparing International Commercial Arbitration Rules* (Sweet & Maxwell, 1998).

There is no requirement that an arbitration be overseen by an arbitral institution. **2.39**
Instead, every international commercial arbitration can be described either as
an institutional arbitration (which is administered by an arbitral institution) or
as an ad hoc arbitration (which is not). Parties to an institutional arbitration
typically pay a fee to the institution based on the amount in controversy that may,
in some instances, exceed the administrative expenses borne by the institution,
and it is this additional cost that leads some parties to avoid institutional arbitration and proceed on an ad hoc basis.[43] Institutional arbitrations are also typically
governed by the rules promulgated by that institution, although there are exceptions to the rule. For example, the LCIA will administer arbitrations under its
own rules or under the UNCITRAL Arbitration Rules or even under a hybrid of
the two.[44]

Parties to an ad hoc arbitration have a great deal of freedom in how they choose **2.40**
to structure their proceedings. In the first place, they need not be subject to any
arbitral rules whatsoever. Instead, they may outline certain procedures in the
arbitration agreement itself or find a way to agree to certain rules of conduct
between themselves after the dispute has arisen. Parties seldom choose to detail
the procedural issues with the same degree of detail as institutional rules, however. Instead, ad hoc arbitrations typically rely on the arbitrator to decide the
procedure in his or her discretion.

However, a completely discretionary proceeding has its downsides, not the least **2.41**
of which is that the parties do not know what to expect when preparing their
cases. Procedural disputes can be chaotic, particularly if the dispute involves
naming or challenging an arbitrator. Parties who wish to avoid these kinds of
uncertainties can opt to have an ad hoc arbitration (in that it is not administered
by an arbitral organization) that is still governed by the procedural rules issued by
an arbitral institution. There is no limitation on the rules that may be chosen to
govern the proceedings and no requirement that there be any link between the
institution that promulgated the rules and the arbitration. Thus, for example,
there is no reason why the LCIA Arbitration Rules cannot be used to govern a
proceeding seated outside the United Kingdom and involving non-English
parties and non-English law. There is also no requirement that the rules be issued
by an international arbitral institution, and indeed some parties may find it
preferable to use a rule set that has been developed in response to the needs of a
particular industry (such as securities brokerages) or that is associated primarily
with domestic litigation. However, because of the unique issues involved in

---

[43] However, as many parties have discovered to their detriment, proceeding on an ad hoc basis
can be a false economy if a problem develops in the proceedings and parallel litigation ensues.
[44] LCIA Rules (n 8), schedule of arbitration fees and costs.

international commercial arbitration, it is likely that rules developed for international disputes are more likely to address all of the necessary concerns.

2.42 One set of rules that has won a large number of adherents among parties to international ad hoc arbitrations is the UNCITRAL Arbitration Rules,[45] promulgated—but not administered—by the United Nations Commission on International Trade Law. The UNCITRAL Arbitration Rules are useful in ad hoc arbitrations for many reasons, not the least of which is that they direct the parties to the Secretary-General of the Permanent Court of Arbitration at The Hague if problems arise with the nomination or challenge of arbitrators.[46] Lack of a nominating authority to decide disputes involving the naming or challenging of arbitrators is one of the downsides of ad hoc arbitrations. While parties to institutional arbitrations can have such issues resolved by the administering agency, parties to ad hoc arbitrations often have to ask for judicial assistance, which can give rise to additional problems ranging from the court's involving itself (unasked) in other aspects of the dispute to questions about the choice of the appropriate forum. Thus the solution used by the UNCITRAL Arbitration Rules—to send parties to the Secretary-General of the Permanent Court of Arbitration at The Hague—is a real step forward.

2.43 The content of the different arbitral rules varies, but one thing is clear—no set of arbitral rules is as comprehensive as the procedural rules contained in national rules of civil procedure. Arbitral rules focus on issues unique to arbitration—procedures for naming, challenging, and replacing arbitrators, for example, or for issuing an arbitral award that is suitable for enforcement. Arbitral rules also typically set forth certain basic parameters that help arbitrators create a procedure that complies with basic principles of due process. However, institutional rules leave the bulk of the actual procedure to the arbitrators to decide, subject to party agreement. Often parties choose one rule set over another because of perceived benefits relating to what is covered in one set of rules versus another. For example, some rule sets provide for expedited proceedings, whereas others explicitly discuss how parties can obtain preliminary relief prior to the naming of the arbitrator who will hear the substantive dispute.[47] However, parties cannot know precisely what an arbitration will look like, simply based on the rule set chosen. Every set of institutional rules gives the arbitrator a great deal of discretion in deciding how the procedural minutiae will play out. Therefore, the parties must be prepared to be flexible when they go into an arbitration.

---

[45] GA Res 31/98, UN Doc A/RES/31/98 (Dec 15, 1976), also available at <http://www.uncitral.org/pdf/english/texts/arbitration/arb-rules/arb-rules.pdf>.

[46] Ibid, arts 6–7.

[47] Compare ICC Rules (n 8), arts 23, 32 and LCIA Rules (n 8), arts 4, 9, 25.

In addition to the various rule sets that address overarching procedural matters, **2.44** there are a growing number of rules promulgated by institutional bodies that address specific subjects related to international arbitration. For example, the International Bar Association ('IBA') has issued the IBA Rules on the Taking of Evidence in International Commercial Arbitration as well as the IBA Guidelines on Conflicts of Interest in International Commercial Arbitration.[48] Other protocols, such as those on the use of electronic evidence, are currently under discussion by some of the leading international arbitral organizations. While neither of these rule sets address procedural issues such as the naming of arbitrators, access to courts, issuance of awards and the like, they are very useful in considering two major areas of potential conflict in arbitration: the taking and presentation of evidence and the challenge of arbitrators. Although few parties will choose to have these rules apply in a pre-dispute arbitration agreement, they can choose to have the rules apply at any time after the arbitration has begun. Similarly, an arbitrator may decide to make these or similar rules applicable, either in their entirety or as general principles.

(5) Sources of law—law of the dispute (procedural orders and agreements between the parties)

As indicated in the preceding section, arbitrators have a great deal of discretion **2.45** in how they shape the arbitral proceedings. Although this discretion can be exercised orally, it is often memorialized in procedural orders that are binding on the parties, just as a judge's procedural orders would be binding in litigation. As such, they can be considered the 'law of the dispute'. The only difference between arbitral and judicial orders is that a procedural order in arbitration can include a number of elements that would normally be covered in litigation by rules of civil procedure and any standing orders of the court. Thus, an arbitrator's procedural orders can include rulings on such matters as the content and form of any necessary pre-hearing submissions, as well as the dates that those submissions are due; orders on the scope of any disclosure that may be needed; the procedure to be used during any oral hearing that may be required, including whether the parties may conduct direct examination of witnesses in lieu of or to supplement written witness statements (as opposed to limiting themselves to cross-examination), and how much time is to be allocated for examination of witnesses versus opening and/or closing argument etc. Because arbitrators' procedural orders are seldom publicized, there is no way to compare content reliably.[49] However, parties can

---

[48] See <http://www.ibanet.org/publications/IBA_Guides_Practical_Checklists_Precedents_and_Free_Materials.cfm>.

[49] Recently, Jan Paulsson wrote an article lauding the procedural orders of highly respected international arbitrator Karl-Heinz Böckstiegel. The article contained the contents of the order, which

expect that many of the procedural rules that will be binding on the parties will be reflected in these sorts of orders.

2.46 Because procedural orders are not published in bound volumes, they may not seem as weighty or important as other forms of arbitral authority, but they are given a great deal of respect in arbitration. Without these orders, the parties would not know how the proceedings would be organized. Furthermore, it may be incumbent upon parties to seek rulings in a timely manner if, for any reason, the arbitrator does not take the initiative to decide critical matters in advance. This may be particularly true if the arbitrator is new to international commercial proceedings.

2.47 The 'law of the dispute' also includes any formal or informal agreements between the parties. While the arbitration agreement constitutes the most important agreement between the parties, there may also be other relevant agreements contained in letters, electronic mails, or other documents.

(6) Sources of law—arbitral awards

2.48 Because international commercial arbitration is a private dispute resolution mechanism that only affects the parties to the arbitration agreement, there is little need to publish arbitral awards, since they typically do not have any precedential value, even in common law jurisdictions, other than for *res judicata* or collateral estoppel purposes. Indeed, the confidential and private nature of arbitration suggests that publication of the award may be improper, although this may be changing.

2.49 Nevertheless, there is a tradition among some of the leading arbitral institutions whereby they publish denatured arbitral awards to give parties some indication on how certain issues have been decided in the past. Although published awards

---

had been reprinted in the award issued in *Tradex Hellas SA v Republic of Albania*, 29 April 1999, 14 ICSID Review—Foreign Investment Law Journal 161 (1999). See Jan Paulsson, 'The Timely Arbitrator: Reflections on the Böckstiegel Method', 22 Arbitration International 19 (2006). See also Karl-Heinz Böckstiegel, 'Major Criteria for International Arbitrators in Shaping an Efficient Procedure', ICC International Court of Arbitration Bulletin, 1999 Special Supplement, 49. The form and contents of typical procedural orders are also discussed by another pre-eminent international arbitrator, Hans Smit, in his article, 'Managing an International Arbitration: An Arbitrator's View', 5 The American Review of International Arbitration 129 (1994). See also Scott Armstrong Spence, 'Organizing an Arbitration Involving an International Organization and Multiple Private Parties: The Example of the Bank for International Settlements Arbitration', 21 Journal of International Arbitration 309 (2004) (discussing content of fourteen different procedural orders); and Rolf Trittmann, 'When Should Arbitrators Issue Interim or Partial Awards and/or Procedural Orders?', 20 Journal of International Arbitration 255 (2003). Sample precedents can also be found in John Tackaberry and Arthur Marriott, *Bernstein's Handbook of Arbitration and Dispute Resolution Practice* (Sweet & Maxwell, 2003).

are not binding on anyone other than the parties, they are persuasive forms of authority, particularly concerning procedural matters that are not typically covered in judicial opinions.[50] Thus, advocates and arbitrators can look to published awards for guidance concerning issues such as the interpretation of arbitral rules, the challenge of arbitrators, permissible procedures in hearings, *compétence-compétence*, and the like.

(7) Sources of law—case law

Common law lawyers are well aware of the importance of case law in deciding legal disputes, since judicial opinions constitute one of the primary sources of law in the common law tradition. If a question (be it substantive or procedural) is governed by the law of a common law jurisdiction, all advocates—no matter whence their legal training—must consult case law when preparing their legal arguments. In those cases, judicial precedents are not simply persuasive authority; they are binding on the arbitrator. **2.50**

There are other times, however, when advocates should consider submitting case law simply for its persuasive power. This is true even when one is not working in the common law tradition. In these instances, the judicial opinion would be submitted to the arbitrator to show that other esteemed decision-makers have decided the issue in a certain way and that their actions suggest—but do not require—a similar outcome in the matter at hand. The most persuasive cases are obviously from the jurisdiction whose law controls the issue in question, since they suggest how courts in that state might review the matter should it come to the courts' attention, but judicial decisions from states where enforcement of the award may be sought are also highly persuasive. In both instances, the arbitrator will be interested in how the courts will consider his or her ruling, since no arbitrator wants to render an unenforceable award. **2.51**

However, arbitrators can also be swayed by judicial opinions from jurisdictions that have no nexus to the dispute or to the parties.[51] This is particularly true when the arbitrator is from a common law jurisdiction, since common law lawyers might be particularly uncomfortable receiving a submission that is based only on statutes, rules, and scholarly commentary. Therefore, advocates who have common law lawyers sitting as arbitrators should take special care to find some sort of **2.52**

---

[50] Because arbitral procedure is left almost entirely to the discretion of the arbitrator, courts very seldom opine on procedural irregularities, unless they are so egregious as to violate basic notions of due process or public policy.

[51] If a state has based its legal system on that of another nation, that other nation's laws and judicial interpretations might also be particularly persuasive. For example, a civil law nation whose code is based on the French model might be more persuaded by the reasoning of a French court than by that of a German or American court.

persuasive case law to support their arguments. The judicial opinion should be on point and discuss the same or similar points of law, but, even more importantly, it should be from a jurisdiction that carries some weight with the arbitrator.

2.53　This leads to the second reason why advocates should consider including case law in their submissions. Quite simply, some jurisdictions are known as leaders in international commercial arbitration due to their longstanding expertise in the field,[52] and opinions from those courts are considered highly persuasive to an arbitrator, regardless of whether the arbitrator is from a common or civil law background. Similarly, decisions from the home jurisdiction of a particular arbitral institution are more likely to be considered persuasive on matters involving those arbitral rules than decisions from other jurisdictions would be. Thus, English cases construing provisions of the LCIA Arbitration Rules are likely to be given more weight than French cases, although French cases will likely be considered more persuasive when the ICC Arbitration Rules are at issue, since the ICC is based in Paris. Furthermore, although an experienced arbitrator will likely take a highly international view of any dispute that he or she is hearing, it is possible that some arbitrators will be swayed by decisions handed down by courts from their home states or by courts in a state that bears a great deal of similarity to their home state.[53] However, there are a growing number of jurisdictions that are gaining expertise in international arbitration, and it may be that an arbitrator finds compelling rationales from courts that bear no connection whatsoever to the dispute at hand. Thus, advocates must be prepared to both advance and defend against case law introduced from a variety of states.

(8) Sources of law—treatises and monographs

2.54　Treatises hold perhaps a unique position of importance in international commercial arbitration. There appears to be two reasons why this is so. First, arbitration is a private affair between the parties, which means that both the disposition of the dispute and the proceedings themselves are typically considered to be confidential. While rules on the extent to which arbitration is confidential may be easing,[54] parties and/or arbitrators still tend to keep the details of an arbitration private.

---

[52] Often, the esteem given to a particular state's judicial opinions matches the state's popularity as a site for international arbitration. Thus, decisions issued by courts in the United Kingdom, France, and Switzerland are considered particularly persuasive, which is reflective of the three states' popularity as arbitral sites. Jan Paulsson, 'Arbitration Friendliness: Promises of Principle and Realities of Practice', 23 Arbitration International 477 (2007).

[53] For example, an arbitrator from a state whose laws are based on the Napoleonic Code might find French law more persuasive than American law or even German law.

[54] See eg, L Yves Fortier, 'The Occasionally Unwarranted Assumption of Confidentiality', 15 Arbitration International 131 (1999); Catherine A Rogers, 'Transparency in International Commercial Arbitration', 54 University of Kansas Law Review 1301 (2006).

Arbitrators' procedural orders are typically not published, and even the denatured final awards that are made available through international arbitral institutions contain very little information about the hearing or pre-hearing proceedings. Thus, there is little in the way of 'public' or easily ascertainable law in this field. To the extent that there is published law, it does not deal with every possible issue or scenario that could arise. For example, arbitral rules and national laws on arbitration may give some broad-brush guidance on procedural points but do not delve into the fine details. Furthermore, although courts are involved in motions to compel arbitration and motions to enforce arbitral awards, very few judicial decisions discuss matters of arbitral procedure.

2.55 As a result, expert commentary holds a special place of prominence on many points of contention simply because there is very little authority available elsewhere. Furthermore, many of the leading commentators have a great deal of practical experience in international arbitration, either as advocates or neutrals, in addition to their scholarly credentials, which gives additional weight to their opinions.

2.56 The second reason why treatises are held in such high esteem relates to the manner in which international commercial arbitration blends civil and common law customs.[55] Lawyers from civil law jurisdictions are well aware of the importance of treatises in forming legal arguments, since expert commentary is often given more respect in civil law litigation than it is in common law litigation. Thus, civil law lawyers are perhaps more likely to include references to treatises in their submissions to the arbitrator than common law lawyers are. Such citations might seem out of place to lawyers from the common law tradition, particularly if other forms of legal authority—such as judicial opinions or statutes—are available. Nevertheless, treatises are a legitimate source of authority in international commercial arbitration and should not be discounted. Therefore, when it comes time to frame their legal arguments, common law lawyers should not hesitate to use treatises to support their arguments, nor should they underestimate the persuasiveness of treatises when used by their opponents.

(9) Sources of law—legal articles

2.57 International commercial arbitration considers scholarly legal articles as almost on a par with legal treatises, with commentary found in reputable peer-reviewed journals specializing in international arbitration being given the most weight. As would be expected, the reputation and credentials of the author factor into the

---

[55] Thus, for example, arbitrators usually schedule oral hearings with the right to cross-examination (both of which are central to the common law tradition) but also give great weight to documentary evidence (which is a trait of the civil law tradition).

determination of how persuasive the piece will be. Because international commercial arbitration is a practical field of inquiry in which many scholars are current or former practitioners, there does not appear to be a wide distinction in persuasiveness between practitioner-authored pieces and scholar-authored pieces. The benefit of legal articles, of course, is that they can: (a) address matters of recent interest in a more timely manner than treatises can; (b) discuss fine points of law in detail; and (c) provide overviews of the state of affairs in jurisdictions where there is not a great deal of authority available, due either to the low number of international arbitrations that take place there or to language issues.

2.58   There are a wide variety of specialty journals available today, and, with the advent of electronic publishing, it has become easier than ever for advocates to conduct research outside their home jurisdictions. Again, however, lawyers have to be prepared to consider certain materials as reputable, even if those materials do not take the same form as those from the lawyers' home jurisdictions. For example, lawyers trained in the United States typically expect a scholarly article to run forty-plus pages in print, with hundreds of footnotes. Anything shorter, or with less visible authority, is considered a legal 'lightweight'. However, non-US lawyers typically view American law review articles—which appear, nearly universally, in student-edited journals—as wordy and not as persuasive as articles that have passed through the peer-review process. Furthermore, scholarly articles published outside the United States are generally much shorter in length (often running no more than ten to fifteen pages in print) with very few footnotes. Nevertheless, these shorter articles carry just as much weight—if not more—with non-US arbitrators, simply because that is how legal scholarship is presented elsewhere in the world.

2.59   Although many of the best articles on international commercial arbitration appear in specialist journals, highly informative analysis can also be found in general journals from around the world. Nowhere is this more true, perhaps, than in the United States, where academics seeking tenure or promotion are pushed to publish in certain high-ranking general law reviews and journals[56] rather than in the type of specialist international journals that might be more likely to be read outside the United States.

---

56 The relative prestige of scholarly journals in the United States is based on the ranking of the law school that sponsors the journal or law review, which is itself reflected in national standings published annually by organizations such as US News & World Report. Furthermore, general (non-subject-matter specific) law reviews are often considered more prestigious than 'specialty' journals. Thus, Harvard Law Review is considered more prestigious than Cornell Law Review (based on relative law school rankings), but Cornell Law Review is more prestigious than Harvard International Law Journal (based on the rule of specialty journals). The merits and content of the ranking system is constantly under debate in the US, but practitioners from outside the US should be aware that some of the best American articles on international commercial arbitration may be found in unexpected sources.

C. How Experienced Advocates Use Legal Authorities

As the preceding discussion suggests, advocates in international commercial **2.60** arbitration must learn to overcome much of the training that they learned in litigation—either national or international—or in domestic arbitration. International commercial arbitration is, quite simply, different than other forms of dispute resolution.

Experienced advocates in this field recognize that legal authorities can come from **2.61** a wide variety of sources. They also understand that what they personally find persuasive may not be considered in the same light by the arbitrator, particularly if that arbitrator comes from a different legal system. Rather than try to force the arbitrator to follow the advocate's view of what the procedure and legal argument should look like, experienced lawyers take an expansive approach to what might be possible, relying on a variety of arguments and authorities and taking into account what their audience—ie, the arbitrator—will find persuasive.

When considering which legal authority should be given the most weight, **2.62** experienced advocates typically start with the agreement between the parties. This can be confusing—although party autonomy is given a great deal of weight in international commercial arbitration and is the starting place for analysis, parties cannot contract out of mandatory provisions of law. Therefore, experienced arbitrators look to the agreement between the parties to identify: (a) the type of arbitration (ad hoc or institutional); (b) whether any institutional rules apply; (c) the location of the arbitration (since that affects which national law affects procedure); (d) any choice of substantive or procedural law; and (e) any specific procedural choices that the parties have made. Although it is not part of the arbitration agreement, experienced advocates also look to where the parties are domiciled and where the parties' assets might possibly be located, since these locations might be the site for a future enforcement action or for a proper (or improper) motion for judicial intervention.

Although the parties' choice will control some issues absolutely,[57] sometimes the **2.63** parties will make a choice that cannot be given effect by the arbitrators. For example, the parties may choose to arbitrate a patent dispute involving a German party, despite the fact that under European Union law, matters involving intellectual property must be heard in the courts. Similarly, parties could attempt to create an arbitral procedure that curtails one of the parties' ability to present its case, which would be a violation of international principles of due process. In neither instance should the arbitrator permit party choice to override mandatory

---

[57] For example, if the parties agree to seat the arbitration in Paris, no court will override that decision.

provisions of relevant law. Sometimes the arbitrator may be able to create a procedure that violates some aspect of the parties' agreement but still yields an enforceable award. Other times the arbitrator may have to cede the matter to the courts. In all cases, advocates need to be aware that mandatory provisions of relevant law trump the parties' agreement, even in a dispute resolution mechanism that touts party autonomy as one of its major benefits.

2.64 Once an experienced advocate has looked at the arbitration agreement to identify the parameters of the arbitration, he or she considers the eight types of legal authority discussed in this chapter. First, the advocate identifies any international instruments—either conventions or treaties—that apply, since the failure to consider enforcement early on may result in an unenforceable award.[58] Furthermore, enforcement conventions—like other sorts of international treaties—typically trump contrary provisions of national law. Because many lawyers do not think to check enforcement requirements until long after the procedure has begun, a wise advocate can sometimes gain tactical advantages by looking ahead to the enforcement stage. If an opponent has failed to comply fully with some necessary element—such as notice—then a lawyer may advise his or her client not to appear in the arbitration, on the theory that even if an award is issued, it will not be internationally enforceable.

2.65 Next, the experienced advocate considers national laws concerning the procedure and substance of the dispute, including, if necessary, any relevant provisions concerning conflict of laws. National laws indicate whether any portion of the dispute must be heard in the courts of any particular country. Additionally, it is important to know if the national statute contains any default provisions on arbitral procedure, since such provisions typically override arbitrator discretion in cases where the parties have not made other wishes known.[59] Again, experienced advocates realize that knowing the elements of every applicable and potentially applicable national law early on can yield tactical advantages. Thus, for example, if there are fundamental problems with the procedure associated with the naming of the arbitrator under the law of the situs, it may make the award unenforceable in that jurisdiction as well as in others.[60] This might lead a party to decide not to appear in the arbitration, since enforcement of any award under domestic or international law will be difficult, if not impossible.

---

[58] In some cases, the international instrument also describes the procedures that the parties must follow in the arbitration itself.

[59] For example, the English Arbitration Act 1996 has a number of potentially surprising default provisions, ranging from the naming of experts, the giving of security, the protection of property, and the dismissal of the arbitration for lack of prosecution. English Arbitration Act 1996, ss 37–8, 41.

[60] See eg, New York Convention (n 5), art V(1)(b), (d).

The next most persuasive form of legal authority typically involves arbitral rules, **2.66** either because the dispute is being administered by a particular institution or because the parties have chosen to use a particular rule set to control an ad hoc proceeding. As a matter of practice, lawyers will (and should) check the relevant arbitral rules and the arbitration agreement the minute that they receive notice that a dispute is pending, since those two sources address many of the immediate questions that arise, but advocates should consult the rules regularly to make sure the proceeding is advancing properly. Although failure to comply with the necessary arbitral rules can lead to an unenforceable award,[61] sitting on a procedural error in the hopes of entering an objection at the enforcement stage could prove risky, since a court could conclude that the failure to object in a timely manner constituted a waiver.

Although procedural orders have a significant impact on how an arbitration is **2.67** conducted, there are no requirements as to when they must be issued, if at all, or what subjects they must cover. Like all other matters involving procedure, issuing orders is entirely within the discretion of the arbitrator. However, a good arbitrator will be responsive to the parties' reasonable requests. Thus, if a decision is needed on a particular subject, the parties should ask for a ruling and an order in writing. Similarly, if the arbitrator does not take the initiative to commit the proposed schedule for submissions and/or hearing dates to writing, the parties should ask for him or her to do so to avoid issues and confusion later on. Advocates should be aware that some arbitrators may resist issuing too many written orders or including their reasons in their orders for fear of having the parties try to appeal the matter to court. As in all areas of arbitration, advocates can make requests but should avoid pushing too hard. Experienced arbitrators know that it is an advocate's job to do all that he or she can to further a client's interests, but it is the arbitrator's responsibility to do what is in the best interest of the arbitration as a whole.

When it comes time to make legal arguments, an experienced advocate looks to **2.68** all available sources of authority—arbitral awards, case law (from any jurisdiction that might prove persuasive to the arbitrator), treatises, and scholarly legal articles—to provide support for his or her position. Though there must be a reasonable legal or factual nexus between the authority offered and the point at issue, providing support from a diverse variety of sources can strengthen an argument by showing international consensus for what is posited. There are, as always, some provisos. For example, American advocates should note that international arbitrators neither favour nor require long 'string cites' (multiple authorities, usually judicial opinions, for the same proposition), despite the fact that string citation remains fairly common in US litigation (though happily diminishing).

---

[61] See eg, New York Convention (n 5), art V(1)(d).

However, an experienced arbitrator would likely look favourably on papers that described why the same outcome would arise based on: (a) commentary contained in a leading treatise; (b) case law arising out of a persuasive jurisdiction; and/or (c) rationales discussed in a published arbitral award. None of these sources is, by itself, determinative, since none of the authorities is binding on the arbitrator, but the fact that a number of persuasive sources have taken a consistent approach to the issue will do much to convince the arbitrator that the position advocated is the one to follow.

D. How Experienced Arbitrators Weigh Legal Authorities

2.69   Those who are new to arbitration sometimes voice concerns about the extent to which the decision-making process reflects 'the law'. Arbitration has gained a bad reputation in some circles based on the supposition that arbitrators simply 'split the baby' (ie, halve the requested relief) regardless of the merits of any legal arguments made. Furthermore, the absence of any type of appellate review gives some parties pause, as does the fact that arbitrators do not even have to be lawyers unless the parties have made such a requirement explicit in their arbitration agreement. As a result, some jurisdictions—most notably the United States— allow 'manifest disregard of law' to act as a basis for setting aside a domestic award,[62] which comforts those who worry about the 'legality' of non-judges acting in a judicial manner while at the same time striking fear in the heart of those who oppose judicial intervention into a procedure that is supposed to be both private and final.

2.70   Inexperienced advocates or parties may have additional concerns if the arbitrator is granted the power to act as an *amiable compositeur* or exercise powers *ex aqueo et bono*. Although both concepts are well defined in international arbitration and create ascertainable standards as to extent to which the arbitrator can or must resort to equitable principles, non-specialists tend to worry that giving an arbitrator one of these powers will result in an award that bears no relation to the merits of the case.

2.71   In fact, most international arbitrators are highly competent and conscientious decision-makers with a great deal of practical experience in law and/or business.

---

[62] See eg, Christopher R Drahozal, 'Codifying Manifest Disregard', 8 Nevada Law Journal 234 (2007). So far, 'manifest disregard of law' has not been upheld in the United States as a permissible objection to the enforcement of a foreign arbitral award under the New York Convention. See Hans Smit, 'Is Manifest Disregard of the Law or the Evidence or Both a Ground for Vacatur of an Arbitral Award?', 8 American Review of International Arbitration 341 (1997). Even if applicable, there is a very difficult burden in proving 'manifest disregard'.

While there are exceptions to the rule, most arbitrators come to the proceedings with the intent and skills to provide a form of dispute resolution that is as good as—if not better than—what one might receive in court.

When deciding a dispute, experienced arbitrators view the hierarchy of authority **2.72** the same way as advocates do, starting with mandatory provisions of national or international law and the agreement of the parties and moving down the chain of persuasiveness in a logical manner. However, advocates always want to know whether there is one source or type of authority that is sure to resonate with an arbitrator in all circumstances.

The answer, of course, has to be 'no'. Arbitrators know that they are subject to two **2.73** external authorities—the agreement of the parties (within the confines permitted) and mandatory provisions of international or domestic law—and always aim to work within the dictates laid down by these two sources. Of course, points may be hotly disputed, but close calls are a part of any dispute resolution process. There is typically no way to control how an arbitrator exercises his or her judgment, just as there is no way to control how a judge exercises his or her judgment. Different people will find different arguments and authorities more persuasive than others. Just as in litigation, advocates can influence the outcome of a dispute through persuasive argument, which includes polished presentation as well as strong research and analysis. However, international commercial arbitration involves at least three difficulties that do not arise in litigation: (1) the procedure tends to involve elements of both common law and civil law traditions, which means that all advocates operate, to some extent, outside the comfort zone of their home systems; (2) many advocates, particularly those who are new to the process, are not familiar with the full range of potential authorities, which includes materials that are not used in domestic arbitration or even in transnational litigation; and (3) arbitrators may not be from the advocates' home states or legal traditions, which can open the door to confusion on the part of the advocates about what the arbitrators expect or want in the way of argument and authority.

Although these difficulties seem daunting, there is much that advocates can do to **2.74** help sway arbitrators to their position. First, advocates can become familiar with the ways in which international commercial arbitration differs from other sorts of dispute resolution so that they can present themselves and their arguments in a manner that is consistent with the expectations of experienced internationalists. Expecting—or worse, insisting—that the arbitral procedure mimic the procedure used in the courts or arbitrations of one's home state diminishes (or even demolishes) an advocate's credibility.

Second, advocates can understand the variety of authority available to them **2.75** and expand their research beyond materials used in domestic dispute resolution.

By showing their facility with a diverse array of sources, advocates not only appear to be the sort of experienced, internationally minded lawyers who know how to conduct themselves in international commercial arbitration, they also put themselves in the position to show that their views are consistent with the leading authorities from a number of jurisdictions. This approach gives the arbitrator some comfort in knowing that adopting that lawyer's position: (1) is in accordance with good international practice, and (2) will likely be recognized as valid in a number of countries, some of which may be asked to enforce the final award.

2.76 Third, advocates can look at the professional background of the arbitrator and try to anticipate—based on the arbitrator's past affiliations and, if relevant, legal training—which types of arguments and authorities will be most persuasive. While a truly international arbitrator will have learned to recognize and respect the validity of many types of source materials, a common law lawyer will, most likely, always have a slightly higher regard for case law than a civil law lawyer will. Conversely, a civil law lawyer will, most likely, give the writings of an esteemed commentator slightly more weight than a common law lawyer, no matter how long he or she has been involved in international arbitration.

2.77 However, there is one more way that advocates can influence the outcome of an arbitral proceeding. Because arbitration is a private form of dispute resolution, the parties often have a role in choosing who hears the dispute. Unlike litigation—in which a judge is assigned to hear the case without any input from the litigants—parties to arbitration often reserve to themselves the right or power to name one or more of the people who will hear the matter. Before naming an arbitrator, advocates can conduct extensive research into candidates' background, not only to identify potential conflicts of interest, but also to identify how the potential arbitrator might analyse different materials in deciding a case. Sometimes an advocate can even interview a potential arbitrator, not to find out how the candidate would decide the issue at hand, but to get an idea of their analytical methods.[63] Experienced international advocates also know that arbitrators have varying degrees of previous experience and come to the dispute with different levels of existing knowledge about certain procedures. An experienced arbitrator can do a lot to guide the parties towards an internationally enforceable award, simply by the way that he or she sets up the procedures. Thus, it may in many cases be better to choose a candidate who has broad experience in international commercial arbitration rather than simply selecting someone who comes from a particular legal system.

---

[63] 'The Art of Arbitrating: Act I Constitution of the Tribunal', 23 Arbitration International 169 (2007).

E. Conclusion

For years, international commercial arbitration has laboured under the reputa-   **2.78**
tion of being something of an insider's club. Certainly, in the past most practitioners and arbitrators did come out of a very few international law firms. With
the explosion in international commerce and investment, however, international
commercial arbitration has become much more prevalent, and many more lawyers now have the opportunity to practise in this area of law.

Although many welcome the entry of international commercial arbitration into   **2.79**
the legal mainstream, it comes at a price. When the practice was limited to a few
elite firms, specialists could ensure that the necessary knowledge was passed on
through one-on-one mentoring and in-house training programs. Nowadays,
generalists leap into the fray, backed by nothing more than perhaps a few continuing legal education seminars. As useful and necessary as those seminars may
be, they cannot make up for years of individualized training, particularly in a field
that is qualitatively different than any other area of law. More is necessary for a
lawyer to represent his or her client well in an international commercial
arbitration.

The first step to becoming a good advocate or arbitrator in international com-   **2.80**
mercial arbitration is to understand the unique strategies used in research and
practice in this field. Therefore, this chapter has discussed: (1) what legal authorities exist in international arbitration; (2) how experienced advocates use those
authorities; and (3) what weight experienced arbitrators give to those authorities.
The next chapter will consider where the necessary legal authorities can be found
and how to use those authorities in practice.

3

RESEARCHING COMMON AREAS
OF DISPUTE

A. Introduction

The preceding chapter described what legal authorities exist in international **3.01** arbitration, how those authorities are used by experienced advocates, and what weight is given to those authorities by experienced arbitrators. This chapter deals with the practicalities of legal research, focusing first on where international commercial arbitration's unique legal authorities can be found and then discussing how to use these materials in some common areas of dispute. In particular, this chapter will describe how to use legal materials when researching:

- arbitration agreements;
- arbitral procedure;
- challenges to an arbitrator; and
- proceedings to recognize, enforce, and challenge an award.

However, before addressing specific problem areas, one needs to understand **3.02** where the relevant materials can be found.

B. Finding Legal Authorities in International Commercial Arbitration

3.03   International commercial arbitration is unique in the legal world. Not only do practitioners and arbitrators have to be familiar with the 'usual' sources of authority (which can come from more than one state) used in litigation, they also have to understand the relevance and use of certain additional sources of law. As discussed in Chapter 2, there are eight categories of legal authority in this area of practice:

- conventions and treaties;
- national laws;
- arbitral rules;
- law of the dispute (procedural orders and agreements between the parties);
- arbitral awards;
- case law;
- treatises and monographs; and
- legal articles.

3.04   Some research techniques are the same as would be used in national or international litigation. Other techniques are unique to the world of international arbitration. We will discuss how to find each type of authority in turn.

(1) Location of law—international conventions and treaties

3.05   International commercial arbitration can invoke international law in several different ways. First, the parties can agree that the substance of the dispute (even disputes between private parties) should be controlled by principles of public international law—ie, the law governing relationships between states—transnational law (such as *lex mercatoria*) or even general principles of law 'recognised by civilized nations'.[1] This type of law can be found in international conventions agreed between states or in international customary law.[2] Methods for locating the source of international conventions or treaties are discussed below.

---

[1] Alan Redfern and Martin Hunter et al, *Law and Practice of International Commercial Arbitration* (Sweet & Maxwell, 2004) paras 101–2, 108–10.

[2] The determination of the content and applicability of customary law is beyond the scope of this text, but the methodology is well discussed in the literature. See eg, Amanda Perreau-Saussine and James Bernard Murphy (eds), *The Nature of Customary Law* (Cambridge University Press, 2007); Mark E Villiger, *Customary International Law and Treaties: A Manual on the Theory and Practice of the Interrelation of Sources* (Kluwer Law International, 1997); Sandeep Gopalan, 'A Demandeur-Centric Approach to Regime Design in Transnational Commercial Law', 39 Georgetown Journal of International Law 327 (2008); Ole Spiermann, 'Twentieth Century Internationalism in Law', 18 European Journal of International Law 785 (2007); Mileno Sterio, 'The Evolution of International Law', 31 Boston College International and Comparative Law Review 213 (2008).

This first type of law is only applicable to an international arbitration if the **3.06** parties so choose. However, there is a second type of international law that constitutes mandatory law, binding on the parties whether or not they have referred to it in their arbitration agreement. This type of law might include investment treaties such as the Convention on the Settlement of Investment Disputes between States and Nationals of Other States ('ICSID Convention')[3] or other bilateral or multilateral investment treaties that require arbitration of disputes. They might also include special-subject arbitration in areas other than international investment. Alternatively, the laws might involve a treaty or convention concerning the international enforcement of an arbitral award, such as the New York Convention, the Geneva Convention, or the Panama Convention.[4]

However, knowing that these sorts of mandatory provisions of international law **3.07** exist is not enough, since an international instrument carries no weight in any particular state (and has no effect on its citizens) until it is signed and ratified by the national legislature. Even then, it typically must wait to be given domestic application, since international instruments are not necessarily self-executing. Therefore, lawyers cannot assume that a particular treaty or convention applies to a particular arbitration, even if the dispute appears to relate to the subject-matter of the dispute, until they have confirmed that the state is a signatory of that instrument and that the provisions are in effect domestically.[5] The matter is further complicated by the fact that some treaties or conventions—most notably, the New York Convention—permit states to make certain reservations when signing onto the agreement, thus diminishing their applicability even further.[6]

Therefore, when considering whether an international convention or treaty **3.08** applies (either as a matter of choice or mandatorily), practitioners should start by obtaining a copy of the document itself and examining its provisions to ascertain whether it applies to the dispute at hand. Many international instruments can be

---

[3] Mar 18, 1965, 575 UNTS 159, TIAS 6090.

[4] Convention on the Recognition and Enforcement of Foreign Arbitral Awards, June 10, 1958, 330 UNTS 3 ('New York Convention'); European Convention on International Commercial Arbitration, Apr 21, 1961, 484 UNTS 364 ('Geneva Convention'); Inter-American Convention on International Commercial Arbitration of 1976, Jan 30, 1975, 14 ILM 336 ('Panama Convention').

[5] Particularly thorny problems regarding the applicability of a convention or treaty can arise in the case of both successor states (ie, when a nation that has signed an international instrument has broken into constituent units or otherwise experienced a fundamental change that calls into question the applicability of an earlier signature or ratification) and post-colonial states (ie, when a former colonial state has achieved independence but has not yet explicitly agreed to adhere to a particular international instrument).

[6] In the case of the New York Convention, the two most important reservations are the limitation of the effect of the convention to commercial matters and the requirement of reciprocity. New York Convention (n 4), art I(3).

found in published treaty series such as the United Nations Treaty Series ('UNTS')[7] or International Legal Materials ('ILM'). As always, lawyers must be sure that they are viewing the most recent version of the instrument and the most recent list of ratifying states.

3.09 Often, researchers can find lists of states that have ratified or acceded to an instrument in the same place that contains the content of the instrument. Alternatively, researchers can look to the national law of the relevant states to identify the extent to which the law has been incorporated into the domestic regime.

3.10 As always in international arbitration, questions will arise as to which states' laws are relevant to the proceeding. That is often a complicated issue, and the answer may vary depending on whether one is discussing the substantive law of the dispute, the procedural law of the dispute, or the law relative to enforcement proceedings. No answer can be given in the abstract, and parties will need to consider the question carefully and strategically.[8]

(2) Location of law—national laws

3.11 In addition to laws regarding a state's accession to an international convention or treaty on arbitration, most states will also have national statutes concerning arbitration. Most lawyers can locate the arbitration law of their home jurisdiction with little difficulty. However, some jurisdictions do not include all relevant provisions concerning arbitration in one place, and this can create problems for foreign lawyers. For example, parties seeking to enforce a foreign arbitral award in the United States need to do more than familiarize themselves with the New York Convention, the Federal Arbitration Act,[9] and the case law construing the two instruments; they must also understand general (ie, unrelated to arbitration) legal provisions regarding both personal and subject-matter jurisdiction under the United States Constitution.[10] While the need to research general laws on jurisdiction might occur to a US lawyer, it is highly unlikely that a foreign lawyer would think it necessary to go beyond the Federal Arbitration Act.[11]

---

[7] The United Nations also makes many of its documents available online at <http://www.un.org/documents>.

[8] See eg, Julian DM Lew et al, *Comparative International Commercial Arbitration* (Kluwer Law International, 2003) paras 17-01 to 18-99; Redfern and Hunter et al (n 1), paras 2-01 to 2-93.

[9] 9 USC § 101 et seq.

[10] See *Glencore Grain Rotterdam BV v Shivnath Rai Harnarain Co*, 284 F3d 114, 1121 (9th Cir 2002); *Base Metal Trading Ltd v OJSC 'Novokuznetsky Aluminum Factory'*, 283 F3d 208, 212 (4th Cir 2002), cert denied, 537 US 822; SI Strong, 'Invisible Barriers to the Enforcement of Foreign Arbitral Awards in the United States', 21 Journal of International Arbitration 479 (2004).

[11] The extent to which the arbitration laws of individual US states are applicable to international arbitration is a matter of some debate. Gary B Born, *International Commercial Arbitration* (Transnational Publishers, 2001) 39–41.

Thus, it is critical to have experienced local counsel whenever one is doing anything more than rudimentary research into the laws of a foreign jurisdiction.

However, there are times when lawyers can conduct adequate independent **3.12** research into the arbitration laws of jurisdictions other than their own.[12] In particular, the advent of electronic research has made it easier to obtain the arbitration laws of foreign states, though researchers need to be careful that they have found all relevant material. It may be that the arbitration law is contained in more than one location (for example, there may be a domestic provision and an international provision, or a general provision and a special-subject provision dealing with a particular area of law, such as consumer protection). Those who are not practitioners in that state might not find all the relevant statutes if they begin with online research. In cases such as these, it might be safer to use hard copy materials, starting with the special loose-leaf services that carry translations of national statutes on arbitration, since they are likely to be more comprehensive.[13] The binders are updated regularly, so there is a relatively low risk of their being out of date.

National laws will, of course, be promulgated by national legislatures and inter- **3.13** preted by national courts. In states with federal structures, practitioners need to understand the interplay between the different constituent jurisdictions.

(3) Location of law—arbitral rules

Of the various types of legal authority used in international commercial arbitra- **3.14** tion, the rules of various arbitral institutions are perhaps the easiest to locate. Usually the rules are available on the arbitral institution's website, sometimes in several different languages. Researchers have to be careful, however, that the rule set that is posted online is that which is referenced in the relevant arbitration agreement; it could be that the agreement refers to the rules that were in effect when the agreement was signed rather than those that are in effect when the dispute arises and/or is filed.

Print versions of arbitral rules are typically easy to obtain as well. First, most arbitral **3.15** institutions provide written copies of their rules free of charge, either upon request or automatically to any parties who appear in an administered arbitration.[14] Second, many of the leading international rules appear in the standard treatises

---

[12] In doing so, one must always be aware of both pragmatic and ethical issues. See eg, Ronald A Brand, 'Uni-State Lawyers and Multinational Practice: Dealing With International, Transnational, and Foreign Law', 21 Vanderbilt Journal of Transnational Law 1135 (2001).

[13] See Chapter 5 under 'National Laws'.

[14] The institution will only send the rules automatically to parties to an administered arbitration; if the parties have chosen to have a certain set of rules govern an ad hoc proceeding, the institution will only send the rules on request, since it cannot know that the arbitration has begun.

used in the field.[15] Compiling commonly used rule sets and national statutes into reference books and loose-leaf binders dates back to the time before the easy (and relatively inexpensive) availability of electronic research. As more advocates and arbitrators turn to online databases for their information, there is less need to have published versions of arbitration statutes and rule sets. Nowadays, such texts are useful for quick reference, but researchers should always check other sources to make sure that the rules have not been updated since the book was published.

(4) Location of law—law of the dispute (procedural orders and agreements between the parties)

3.16 The term 'law of the dispute' refers to those agreements and provisions that are unique to the particular arbitration at hand. These authorities are not published in books or on websites, but instead consist of the arbitration agreement between the parties (which can arise either before or after the dispute) and any procedural orders issued by the arbitrator. Notably, an arbitration agreement need not be titled as such or be included within the substantive contract between the parties for it to be binding. There have even been instances when an agreement to arbitrate has been contained in a document that was not signed by a party that is to be bound by that agreement.[16] Furthermore, advocates need to keep abreast of any informal agreements between the parties that may be memorialized in letters or electronic mails. Similarly, there are times when an arbitrator will make a binding procedural decision either orally or in a document that is not presented as a formal procedural order. Parties need to be aware of any potential gray areas and seek a ruling in questionable cases.

(5) Location of law—arbitral awards

3.17 Many newcomers to international commercial arbitration have difficulty not only finding arbitral awards issued in other arbitrations, but understanding their value. Although a previously issued arbitral award does not bind the arbitrators or the parties in unrelated disputes (and thus does not constitute legal precedent), these awards can prove highly persuasive. In many ways, these awards are most influential in matters involving arbitral procedure, since those issues typically do not end up in national courts and thus are not often discussed juridically.

---

[15] See eg, Eric E Bergsten, International Commercial Arbitration (Oxford University Press, loose-leaf); Redfern and Hunter et al (n 1); John Tackaberry and Arthur Marriott, *Bernstein's Handbook on Arbitration and Dispute Resolution Practice* (Sweet & Maxwell, 2003).

[16] There are several ways in which a non-signatory may be bound to an agreement to arbitrate. See eg, Lew et al (n 8), paras 7-33 to 7-58; 16-50; 16-70 to 16-78; 17-8 to 17-10; and 17-22 to 17-26.

However, arbitral awards can address a wide variety of subject-matters and should be consulted in many different circumstances.

Arbitral awards are as easy to research as case law, once one knows where to look. **3.18**
Before electronic research became the norm, arbitral awards were only available in certain specialist publications.[17] Although these periodicals and loose-leaf binders continue to be available in printed form, many are also available electronically— either through CD-ROMs or online—typically through various commercial databases.[18] The awards are published without information that could identify the parties and cover a variety of issues ranging from procedural disputes to jurisdictional matters to decisions on the merits. Both electronic and printed awards are indexed for ease of use.

(6) Location of law—case law

In some jurisdictions, case law forms a centrepiece of the national legal order, **3.19**
while in other jurisdictions, it holds more of an ancillary role. Nevertheless, case law can be persuasive, even to arbitrators from jurisdictions that do not traditionally hold case law in high regard, because it gives the arbitrator some idea of: (a) how other experienced legal minds have handled the issue, and (b) how a particular court will view an arbitral decision, should it be challenged in that jurisdiction. Similarly, courts that have not faced a particular issue before may find judicial opinions from other jurisdictions useful in determining the proper course of action. This is particularly true if the court is interpreting a provision based on the UNCITRAL Model Law, since courts often recognize that some degree of international consistency in the interpretation of domestic formulations of the Model Law is desirable, though not always possible or put into action.

Several of the leading arbitral reporting series (both electronic and print) carry **3.20**
judicial opinions on international arbitration.[19] Many of these decisions appear

---

[17] Some of the hard copy compilations of arbitral awards include the ASA Bulletin (Wolters Kluwer Law & Business, periodical); Collection of ICC Awards/Recueil des sentences arbitrales de la ICC (Kluwer Law & Taxation, series); Roger Alford (ed), World Trade and Arbitration Materials (Kluwer Law International, series); Sigvard Jarvin and Annette Magnusson (eds), *SCC Arbitral Awards 1999–2003* (Juris Publishing, 2006); and Albert Jan van den Berg (ed), Yearbook Commercial Arbitration (Kluwer Law International, loose-leaf).

[18] Some subscription databases include Westlaw, LexisNexis, arbitrationlaw.com, and Kluwer Arbitration. Free online sources include the award site for decisions arising out of the Convention on the Settlement of Investment Disputes between States and Nationals of Other States ('ICSID Convention') at <http://icsid.worldbank.org/ICSID/Index.jsp> and the UNCITRAL award site at <http://www.uncitral.org/>, which includes case law on UNCITRAL texts ('CLOUT') and annotations to the UNCITRAL Model Law on International Commercial Arbitration Law.

[19] See Chapter 5 under 'Case Law'.

in English and/or French, the two primary languages of international commercial arbitration, although some of the cases appear only in abstract form.

3.21 It has always been possible to undertake independent legal research in the national reporters of one's home system as well as foreign legal systems, so long as one had sufficient access to the materials and adequate language skills. For better or worse, electronic databases have increased the likelihood that practitioners will attempt to research case law in a jurisdiction other than their own. However, lawyers should be careful about attempting independent research in a jurisdiction other than their own, even if there are no apparent language issues. Every legal system is different, and even though concepts and terms of art may seem similar, there is no guarantee that 'false friends' will not arise.[20]

(7) Location of law—treatises and monographs

3.22 Treatises are, quite often, the easiest way to begin research, and practitioners in this area of law are fortunate to have a number of excellent works available both in print and electronically. However, every text bears the hallmarks of its author's national perspective, so a wise lawyer looks at several different sources during his or her research. In this area of law in particular, much can be learned by looking at an issue from differing viewpoints rather than relying only on one or two treatises that are written from the perspective of one's home jurisdiction.

3.23 Treatises focusing on domestic arbitration also exist in most jurisdictions. These domestic resources can, in many cases, be invaluable when investigating procedural and substantive issues regarding national treatment of issues such as the competence of the arbitrator to decide his or her own jurisdiction, interim judicial assistance, and actions to enforce or set aside an award. While one must always be careful to identify differences between provisions relating solely to domestic arbitration and provisions relating to international arbitration, these resources are nevertheless critical to understanding the intricacies of a particular jurisdiction.

3.24 At one time, the primary type of monograph in international commercial arbitration was the 'soup to nuts' general treatise covering each of the major issues that a practitioner might face during the course of an arbitration. As this area of law has matured, however, detailed single-issue monographs have proliferated, addressing a wide variety of subjects with a great deal of depth. This increase in resources is both a benefit and a curse. Researchers now have more authorities at their disposal but also have to deal with the growing number of debates that

---

[20] For a discussion of the usefulness and limits of comparative legal research, see Konrad Zweigert et al, *An Introduction to Comparative Law* (Oxford University Press, 1998).

scholarly commentary engenders. With the diversification of viewpoints it also is becoming more difficult for newcomers to the field to identify who the leading voices are.

Treatises and monographs are available for purchase commercially, and the titles **3.25** can often be found through online searches. They can also be found in many university law libraries and through subscription-based electronic databases.

(8) Location of law—legal articles

Legal articles appear in a variety of sources, ranging from traditional legal periodi- **3.26** cals, specialist publications, and books containing collections of articles. The relative value of a legal article depends on the qualifications of the author(s), the rigour of the research and writing, as well as the reputation of the publication itself. However, there are differing views as to which publications are the most authoritative.

While a number of leading practitioners and academics in the field publish **3.27** nearly exclusively in the top peer-reviewed journals, excellent articles can and do appear in general legal publications as well. This is particularly true of articles written by American authors, who gravitate towards the student-edited journals published by the more than 170 law schools in the United States.[21] Because the general law journals are often considered more prestigious in the United States than the specialty international journals, some of the best US articles on international commercial arbitration appear in non-specialist publications. The same can be true in other jurisdictions, where there are fewer journals available for legal scholarship.

Furthermore, articles on international commercial arbitration are not limited to **3.28** traditional legal journals. Because this area of practice requires the broad dissemination of a wide variety of specialist-specific information, a number of compilation publications exist that include legal commentary along with information on arbitral awards, arbitral rules, and law from foreign jurisdictions. Researchers need to be sure to consult these sources, which are published anywhere from periodically to annually.

Articles can also appear in collections of related works. Some of these collections will **3.29** be published by commercial publishers, while others will be put out by non-profit

---

21 The fact that the vast majority of academic legal periodicals in the United States are student-run rather than peer-reviewed should not cause those outside the United States undue concern; for the most part, the articles are rigorously researched (as demonstrated by the US footnoting convention, which seems excessive to those outside the US but which shows the author's depth of knowledge) and present reputable legal arguments despite the absence of any peer review in the selection process.

organizations and other international institutions interested in disseminating information about international commercial arbitration and related fields.

3.30 Although research in printed works has its own issues, providers of some electronic databases have tried to make the task of finding relevant information easier by promoting specialized 'international' search fields. While some of these databases—particularly those that are compiled by publishers specializing in international law or international arbitration—are useful to researchers, newcomers to the field need to review the content of the resources before relying on these sorts of designations. In some cases, editors have simply lumped any journal with the word 'international' into the database, despite the fact that many worthwhile articles appear in general journals.

C. Researching Common Areas of Interest in International Commercial Arbitration

3.31 Every question of law is different, and there is no way to know in advance precisely how a research strategy will unfold. However, over time, experienced lawyers learn certain shortcuts that yield useful information quickly and efficiently. This is particularly true in a field like international commercial arbitration, which includes not only unusual legal concepts but also unusual legal resources.

3.32 The novelty of the resources in international commercial arbitration has an impact on a lawyer's research methods. Other areas of law use the same resources regardless of the subject-matter of the inquiry, thus allowing researchers to use similar strategies regardless of the issue at hand. Those who work in international commercial arbitration have to use different research methodologies according to the type of question presented. Sometimes, for example, an investigation needs to focus primarily on national law, whereas at other times the researcher has to seek answers in treatises or arbitral awards.

3.33 While it is impossible to provide detailed guidance on how to proceed on every issue that could arise in international commercial arbitration, the following discussion is intended to provide some structure to the research efforts of those who are new to the field and demonstrate how research strategies evolve. Particular emphasis is given to areas that arise repeatedly over time, though readers are cautioned to always rely on their own professional judgment when considering any legal problem.

3.34 Among the more common questions in an international commercial arbitration are those involving:

- arbitration agreements;
- arbitral procedure;

- challenges to an arbitrator; and
- recognition, enforcement, and challenge of an award.

The following discussion addresses each in turn.

(1) Researching arbitration agreements

Issues involving arbitration agreements can arise at two separate times. First, **3.35** lawyers are often asked, even before a dispute arises,[22] whether arbitration is a suitable dispute resolution mechanism and, if so, what the arbitration agreement should provide. This kind of anticipatory research focuses on finding the most suitable arbitration procedures for any dispute arising out of a contract, although the precise parameters of the dispute will not yet be known. Lawyers doing this kind of research always need to remember that the requirements for a valid arbitration agreement may differ depending on whether the dispute is domestic or international.[23]

Second, lawyers will be asked to research questions about an existing arbitration **3.36** agreement after a dispute arises. Here, advocates and arbitrators must consider matters such as: (a) whether the dispute is covered by the arbitration agreement; (b) what procedures have been agreed by the parties; and (c) whether and what kind of constraints have been placed on the arbitrator.

(a) Research when drafting arbitration agreements

All contracts, no matter how simple, should include a dispute resolution clause. This **3.37** is particularly true, however, if there are trans-border elements to the transaction. Some parties or lawyers prefer to avoid such clauses, either because the negotiation process is already complex or because the parties don't think a dispute will ever arise, but that strategy is penny wise and pound foolish, given how intricate (and expensive) the international dispute resolution process is. At a minimum, every international contract needs to contain a choice of substantive governing law for the dispute and a choice of forum. The choice of forum provision can indicate that a particular national court will hear any eventual disputes or that the parties are to take some or all of their disputes to arbitration.[24] Viewing the dispute resolution clause as a choice of forum rather than an arbitration agreement helps the drafting lawyer recognize that he or she always needs to consider whether arbitration

---

[22] Although it is possible to draft an arbitration agreement after a dispute has arisen, the negotiation process can be lengthy (particularly if the dispute is particularly contentious) and may need to take account of additional considerations. See eg, Redfern and Hunter et al (n 1), paras 3-57 to 3-59.

[23] See eg, Lew et al (n 8), paras 7-11 to 7-18.

[24] Parties can also utilize other forms of alternative dispute resolution, including mediation or conciliation, either separately or in connection with litigation or arbitration.

is even appropriate in the circumstances at hand. Though arbitration—particularly in the international realm—has a great many advantages, it is not always the best means of resolving differences between parties. While it is true that it is easier to enforce an arbitral award internationally than it is to enforce a judgment of court, that cannot be the only concern. A drafter must also consider the type of disputes that may arise (particularly since some may be non-arbitral) and whether it is wise to address any or all of them in arbitration; the location and availability of evidence (since arbitration and litigation take different approaches to disclosure/discovery, and one may want to obtain or block access to certain items); whether there is a need for interim relief, particularly in the time before an arbitrator can be named; and other business and tactical issues.[25]

3.38 Once the parties have agreed that they want to arbitrate any disputes that may arise, they need an appropriate agreement. Some concerns—such as the number of arbitrators, the method of appointment,[26] qualifications for arbitrators, the language of the arbitration and any procedural requirements—are entirely pragmatic and typically do not require legal research per se (though they require forethought and planning).[27] However, lawyers may need to investigate issues such as:

- whether any of the potentially relevant national laws[28] put any limitations on the parties' agreement to arbitrate;

- how potentially relevant national laws interpret language concerning the scope of an arbitration agreement;

- whether any potentially relevant national laws take an unusual stance regarding the finality and/or registration of the award;[29]

---

[25] A full discussion of these issues is outside the scope of this text, but further information can be found at Born (n 11), 7–11; Lew et al (n 8), paras 1-13 to 1-31; Redfern and Hunter et al (n 1), paras 1-41 to 1-68; David St John Sutton et al, *Russell on Arbitration* (Sweet & Maxwell, 2007) paras 1-022 to 1-032.

[26] However, if the arbitration is to proceed under a particular rule set, parties should be aware that the chosen rules may include a default provision regarding appointment procedures, should the parties fail to agree explicitly on another method.

[27] For example, parties may explicitly require a hearing, insist upon the use of the IBA Guidelines on the Taking of Evidence in International Commercial Arbitration, make arrangements for the possibility of consolidation and/or multiparty arbitration, etc.

[28] The question of what national laws are 'potentially relevant' to any issue in an international commercial arbitration can be incredibly complex. Up to nine different approaches have been used in practice. Marc Blessing, 'The Law Applicable to the Arbitration Clause and Arbitrability: Academic Solutions versus Practice and "Real Life"', ICCA Congress Series No 9, 169 (1998).

[29] At one time, US courts required language in the arbitration agreement concerning the binding and final nature of any award issued out of the arbitration as well as the entry of judgment in a competent court, but that may have changed in recent years. See Born (n 11), 889–90 and n 45. Nevertheless, it is still recommended that parties who anticipate possible enforcement of the award in the United States include language regarding the 'final and binding' nature of the arbitration as well as language to the effect that 'judgment upon the award rendered by the arbitrators may be entered in any court having jurisdiction'. See Born (n 11), 889; Dana H Freyer, 'Practical Considerations in

- whether any potentially relevant national laws take an unusual stance regarding the enforceability of the award (which can involve access to courts[30] or interpretation of the relevant grounds for objection to enforcement of awards[31]);

- whether one arbitral rule set is more appropriate for this dispute than another;[32] and

- whether one state is a more appropriate seat for this arbitration than another.

Several of these issues can use the same research strategy. For example, any inquiries into any potentially relevant national laws will focus on the statutes and cases of each of the various jurisdictions. The important thing in these cases is to look beyond one's own national boundaries. Even if the assumption is that the arbitration will be seated in one's home jurisdiction and controlled both procedurally and substantively by one's own national law, it is still necessary to consider how the issue could or would be treated elsewhere. For example, it may be that seating the arbitration in another jurisdiction will result in a procedural advantage that benefits your client. Alternatively, you may discover that enforcement issues will arise if you make one—but not another—issue arbitrable or if you permit the arbitrator to award punitive damages (common in the US but not common—and not considered proper—in many other countries). There are a multitude of issues that can be avoided when the arbitration agreement is in the drafting stages.   **3.39**

Because the questions are—at this point—relatively general, so, too, is the necessary research. National statutes on arbitration appear in specialized arbitral resources and on electronic databases, both free and subscription-based. Law review articles and treatises can also give an overview of arbitration in jurisdictions other than one's own, which can be helpful since there may be some issues that may not appear on the surface of the relevant statutes.   **3.40**

When considering which arbitral rules to choose (if any), newcomers to this area of law must remember that arbitration allows drafters to mix and match   **3.41**

Drafting Dispute Resolution Clauses in International Commercial Contracts: A US Perspective', 15 Journal of International Arbitration 7 (1998); John M Townsend, 'Drafting Arbitration Clauses: Avoiding the 7 Deadly Sins', 58 Dispute Resolution Journal 28 (Feb–Apr 2003).

[30] For example, US law requires certain jurisdictional tests to be met before an enforcement action can be heard. See eg, Strong (n 10).

[31] For example, much has been made of whether 'manifest disregard of law' is a permissible objection in the United States to the enforcement of a foreign award under the New York Convention. See eg, Troy L Harris, 'The "Public Policy" Exception to Enforcement of International Arbitration Awards Under the New York Convention With Particular Reference to Construction Disputes', 24 Journal of International Arbitration 9, 17 (2007).

[32] Though many arbitral rules are similar in many regards, there are variations that can be important to parties. For more on the differences between individual rule sets, see Simpson, Thacher & Bartlett LLP, *Comparison of International Arbitration Rules* (Juris Publishing, 2002); Hans Smit, *A Chart Comparing International Commercial Arbitration Rules* (Sweet & Maxwell, 1998).

different elements. For example, there is no requirement that there be any nexus between the seat of an arbitration and the arbitral rules chosen to govern the arbitral procedure. Similarly, there is no requirement that an arbitration that is administered by a particular institution must be seated in the jurisdiction where the institution is based. Therefore, while it is true that many ICC arbitrations are seated in France (which is where the ICC is based) and many AAA arbitrations[33] are seated in the United States (since the AAA is an American institution), that same ICC arbitration could just as easily be seated in Australia, while the AAA arbitration could be seated in Turkey. Furthermore, none of these choices need to correspond to the controlling substantive law. Quite simply, parties can create the combination of arbitral seat, procedures, rules, and laws that suits them best. While parties may choose to have their arbitration seated in the location whence the applicable rule set arises because they believe (often rightfully so) that there is more case law construing those rules in that jurisdiction and thus more predictability, some other formulation may work better for reasons unique to these parties.

3.42   When considering the different arbitral rules, it's often easiest to look up the most recent version of the rules on the institutional website, though there are also many print resources available. Should the parties wish to invoke a certain set of institutional rules, finding appropriate language for the arbitration agreement is very simple. In addition to the rules themselves, most arbitral institutions provide sample clauses that can be inserted in an arbitration agreement to invoke that particular rule set, whether or not the arbitration will be administered by the institution. Parties should follow these clauses as closely as possible. While some individualization may and often will be necessary,[34] the core clause—that which invokes the rules themselves and/or the administrative function of the institution—should be as suggested by the institution, since any deviation from the standard clause could raise questions about the proper construction of the clause. However, drafters must be careful not to create conflicts and issues when individualizing their arbitration agreement; failure to understand how one modification affects another part of the agreement can have disastrous effects.[35]

---

[33] The AAA's international division is known as the International Centre for Dispute Resolution ('ICDR').

[34] For suggestions on the type of issues that can be addressed in an arbitration agreement, see Redfern and Hunter et al (n 1), paras 8-20 to 8-73; Stephen R Bond, 'How to Draft an Arbitration Clause', 6 Journal of International Arbitration 65 (1989); and Dr Iur Oliver Dillenz, 'Drafting International Commercial Arbitration Clauses', 21 Suffolk Transnational Law Review 221 (1998). At the very least, the parties must include three essential elements to create a proper arbitration agreement—language indicating the agreement to arbitrate and the scope of the agreement as well as provisions regarding the finality of the award. See eg, Lew et al (n 8), para 8-09.

[35] For example, indicating two or more different authorities as being simultaneously competent to appoint arbitrators would create a conflict that would doubtless end up in dispute and could even lead to the nullification of the arbitration agreement.

(b) Research involving existing disputes

Research relating to the drafting of an arbitration agreement is often relatively **3.43** general, since the parties do not know what future disputes will arise and are trying to create an optimal process for a variety of possible eventualities. Once an actual dispute arises, the research becomes much more specific, and the research strategy narrows accordingly. Advocates use the same sources described above— national law, arbitral rules, legal commentary, etc—but do not look to see which offers the best possible outcome. Instead, their research is constrained by the terms of the arbitration agreement and the facts of the case.

This does not mean that there is not room for comparative legal research and **3.44** creative lawyering. First, the parties may disagree about what the arbitration agreement actually says. For example, one side may argue that the law of country X controls either the substance or the procedure of the dispute, whereas the other side argues that the law of country Y controls. No capable advocate would make these arguments without having researched the law of country X and Y in advance to make sure that the position taken actually benefited his or her client. Second, the parties should always look to other jurisdictions to identify persuasive authority that supports their position or weakens their opponent's position. Comparative legal research is uniquely persuasive in international commercial arbitration, though perhaps especially concerning matters of procedure.

Research regarding the arbitration agreement can arise at any time during the **3.45** proceedings. Typical questions might include: (a) whether the arbitration agreement is binding; (b) whether the arbitration agreement covers the dispute that has arisen; (c) whether the procedure that was used was contemplated by the arbitration agreement; and/or (d) whether the arbitrator is competent to decide his or her own jurisdiction.

(2) Researching arbitral procedure

Researching arbitral procedure can be difficult. Because arbitration is intended to **3.46** be a flexible and pragmatic dispute resolution process, arbitrators have a great deal of discretion in how to shape the proceedings. Furthermore, the confidential nature of arbitration means that few details about previous proceedings are made public. Even within the general field of international commercial arbitration, there may be variations in procedure based on the type of dispute that is at issue.[36] Therefore, parties can find it difficult to predict how their arbitration will proceed, and courts can have trouble identifying the standards that should be

---

[36] See eg, Karl-Heinz Böckstiegel, 'The Role of Arbitrators in Investment Treaty Arbitration', *ICCA Congress Series No 11* (Kluwer Law International, 2003) 366, 373–4.

used to vacate or refuse enforcement of an award as a result of procedural impropriety.

3.47 Not only is there a dearth of published information on arbitral procedure, but many who are new to the field will look for that information in the wrong places. Often, non-specialists start their research on arbitral procedure by looking at what is done in the national courts, based on the belief that the two procedures are or should be similar.[37] However, only some elements—usually only those relating to mandatory principles of law such as the core elements of due process—carry over from judicial dispute resolution into arbitration. Even then, the question arises as to which national law should apply.

3.48 However, many procedural questions do not rise to the level of mandatory law. In those cases, the question may be addressed by national law, or it may not. The research strategy to follow in these instances follows the hierarchy of legal authority. The first level of authority—mandatory provisions of law—appears not to apply. Therefore, the question is whether the parties have agreed to a certain procedure. To answer that question, one must look at the arbitration agreement and any institutional rules or guidelines that are incorporated by reference into the arbitration agreement. Next, the researcher should see how those rules or guidelines have been construed, either by the national court whose law controls the issue, or by other courts whose views might be persuasive. It may be that the parties have to argue by analogy, since it is possible that the precise wording of the arbitration agreement may not have been judicially discussed yet. Next, the researcher should look at arbitral awards that have been published in any specialized databases or compilations. It may be that an arbitrator has discussed certain aspects of arbitral procedure in a published award or interim order.

3.49 If these methods do not provide clear guidance—and it is very possible that they will not, since arbitral procedure is seldom discussed in case law or awards in any detail—then the researcher must look to treatises and other scholarly writings. Because treatises and legal articles tend to speak in general, rather than specific, terms, advocates may have to argue by analogy and from general principles, although there is nothing inherently difficult or unusual about that. Finally, parties can look to arbitral rule sets and specialized guidelines (such as the IBA

---

[37] The emphasis on national procedure may also be based on the fact that challenges regarding arbitral procedure will often be made in domestic courts as part of a motion to vacate an award or as an objection to its international enforcement. However, it is well established that international arbitrators have both the discretion and the duty to deviate from national law or procedure, although debate exists as to the extent to which such deviation is proper. See eg, Guillermo Aguilar Alvarez, 'To What Extent Do Arbitrators in International Cases Disregard the Bag and Baggage of National Systems?', *ICCA Congress Series No 8* (Kluwer Law International, 1996) 139.

Guidelines on the Taking of Evidence in International Commercial Arbitration for questions regarding the introduction of evidence) that are not binding on the parties but that help suggest what constitutes good arbitral procedure. While there is no established 'customary law' of arbitration, one can make an argument that a consensus of learned practitioners can yield a 'best practice' in the field and that any significant deviation from that practice would not be within the reasonable contemplation of the parties at the time the arbitration agreement was signed.

Although conventions and treaties do not provide much assistance to any discussion of arbitral procedure, they sometimes play a background role in this area of law. For example, a party may need to cite the appropriate provision in a treaty or convention that indicates that a failure to comply with proper arbitral procedure (typically defined as 'the agreement between the parties'[38]) will support an objection to the international enforcement of an arbitral award. **3.50**

(3) Researching challenges to the arbitrator

Another common question that can cause problems for researchers who do not specialize in international commercial arbitration involves challenges to the arbitrator.[39] First, the procedure itself is often difficult to fathom and can vary depending on which arbitral rules (if any) govern the arbitration. Second, the standards for determining whether a challenge should be upheld are not typically found in the resources that non-specialists are most familiar with, ie, national law. Instead, researchers must consult special arbitral resources and databases if they want to present a well-supported submission to the decision-maker. **3.51**

To understand how to find resources discussing challenges, one must understand how and when a challenge can come about. Essentially, a challenge to an arbitrator can arise at three different points in time: (1) at the beginning of the arbitration, when the arbitrator is first named; (2) in the middle of the arbitration; and (3) at the end of the arbitration, after the hearing and/or after the award has been issued. At all three times, the arbitrator may be challenged for lack of independence,[40] **3.52**

---

[38] See eg, New York Convention (n 4), art V(1)(d).

[39] Experienced practitioners spend a great deal of time selecting any party-appointed arbitrators, since it is commonly believed that having the right arbitrator(s) will do much to ensure a positive outcome for one's client. A detailed discussion of the means used to research an arbitrator's background is beyond the scope of this text, but there are resources available that can help parties identify potentially appropriate choices. See eg, *Guide to the World's Leading Experts in Commercial Arbitration* (Expert Guides, 2006); *Martindale-Hubbell International Arbitration and Dispute Resolution Directory* (Reed Business Information Inc, 2008); Hans Smit and Vratislav Pechota (eds), The Roster of International Arbitrators (Juris Publishing, loose-leaf). Martindale-Hubbell's online database can be found at <http://dispute.martindale.com/index.php>.

[40] The terminology in this area of law can be confusing. The international literature speaks of the need for arbitrators to be both independent and impartial, though some national laws do not

meaning that the arbitrator has some personal, professional, or financial connection to the parties, the lawyers representing the parties, or the dispute itself that results in an actual or potential conflict of interest.[41]

3.53   Once the arbitration has begun, it is possible for a party to enter a challenge based on the arbitrator's perceived lack of impartiality, meaning that the arbitrator has demonstrated some sort of bias on behalf of one of the parties, either giving one side positive preferential treatment or curtailing the other side in some way. Evidence of bias can range from the type of questions the arbitrator poses to a witness (or allows a lawyer to pose or not to pose) to rulings on the admission of evidence to an arbitrator's general demeanour. In most cases, a challenge must be made within a certain amount of time after the party has learned of the offending behaviour or relationship, since the international arbitral community frowns on delayed objections which may only be raised if and when a party loses the dispute on the merits or as a delaying tactic.

3.54   When contemplating a challenge, the party must first identify the authority to which the challenge should be made. If the arbitration is administered, the challenge is typically addressed to the arbitral institution pursuant to the procedure outlined in the institutional rules. Arbitrations that are not administered by an institution may sometimes also submit a challenge to such an institution, although a fee will be charged to offset the cost of hearing the challenge.[42] This typically would occur if the parties have chosen to have their ad hoc proceeding governed by the rules of a particular institution. Arbitrations that proceed under the UNCITRAL Arbitration Rules typically submit challenges to the Secretary-General of the Permanent Court of Arbitration at The Hague in accordance with articles 6–7, 11, and 12 of the UNCITRAL Arbitration Rules.[43] Some ad hoc arbitration agreements will indicate expressly how a challenge is to be heard. For example, some may indicate that any challenge is to be heard by the

---

require both. Furthermore, there is some dispute about whether an international arbitrator also needs to be 'neutral', which may not be required in some domestic arbitrations. See generally Lew et al (n 8), paras 13-8 to 13-18; Redfern and Hunter et al (n 1), paras 4-52 to 4-64.

[41] A discussion of actual versus potential conflicts of interest is beyond the scope of this discussion, but there are numerous treatises and guidelines on the subject. The most persuasive provisions are found in the International Bar Association Guidelines on Conflicts of Interest in International Arbitration, published in 2004, but researchers can also consult the American Arbitration Association Code of Ethics for Arbitrators in Commercial Disputes of 2004 and the International Bar Association Rules of Ethics for International Arbitrations of 1986. See also Catherine Rogers, *Ethics in International Arbitration* (Oxford University Press, 2009).

[42] See eg, <http://www.lcia-arbitration.com/> (indicating the LCIA will hear challenges even in non-LCIA arbitrations for a fee).

[43] The UNCITRAL Arbitration Rules are not institutional rules, per se, since UNCITRAL does not administer arbitrations in the same way that institutions like the ICC, the LCIA, or the AAA do.

Secretary-General of the Permanent Court of Arbitration at The Hague, even if the UNCITRAL Arbitration Rules are not binding on the parties, whereas others will require a challenge to be heard in the national courts of a particular country, which would usually (but not necessarily) be the seat of the arbitration.[44]

If the arbitration agreement does not incorporate a rule set that has its own built-in challenge procedure and does not otherwise indicate how a challenge is to be heard, parties have to bring the challenge in court. Typically national statutes on arbitration include some provision on how a challenge can be brought in the national courts, although those statutes—like arbitral rules—do not provide any detailed standards under which the merits of the challenge are to be evaluated.[45]   **3.55**

Because so many challenges to arbitrators are brought privately, national case law provides little assistance to those who are considering bringing or defending a challenge to an arbitration. National statutes on arbitration are equally unhelpful, since they focus on the challenge procedure rather than the merits of a challenge. Therefore, advocates must look elsewhere when searching for information on whether an arbitrator has acted improperly. There are three types of resources that should be consulted on questions involving a challenge to the arbitrator.   **3.56**

First, advocates must consult the specialized arbitration resources—both electronic and traditional—that carry arbitral reports and awards. This is an area where arbitral institutions want to create some degree of international consistency, since it is in everyone's best interests to know what types of relationships and behaviours can result in a successful challenge, so every year more reports on challenges are published by the institution. Although there is no 'precedent' in arbitration, the most persuasive decisions come from the same institution that is to decide one's own challenge procedure, possibly because there is a sense that each institution has its own implicit or explicit internal standards on what constitutes challengeable behaviour. However, since there are not many reported decisions available, factual similarities to the situation at hand—rather than the identity of the arbitral institution that heard the challenge—will likely be the most important factor, which means that researchers should consider reports from any international institution, no matter where it is located. It doesn't matter whether the challenge will be heard by an arbitral institution or a judge—arbitral reports and awards are persuasive in both contexts, since they provide detailed descriptions of the kinds of behaviour and relationships that those in the international arbitral   **3.57**

---

[44] Parties who choose to include an individualized challenge procedure in their arbitration agreements must, of course, be sure that the body that is designated to hear the challenge is amenable to acting in that capacity.

[45] See eg, Federal Arbitration Act (US), §§ 5, 206, 303; Arbitration Act 1996 (England), ss 16–27.

community find problematic. In fact, because many courts view their role as limited to upholding the parties' expectations about the type of dispute resolution procedure in which they have agreed to participate, the views of the arbitral community are often considered highly persuasive.[46]

3.58 Second, researchers must look to the work of learned scholars and respected practitioners. Because parties to an arbitration agreement are considered to have contracted for a procedure that is in accordance with international commercial custom, the views of acknowledged experts in the field are considered highly relevant. There are two different places to find relevant authority. The first is in treatises and scholarly journals. As always, one should both expand the search beyond one's national borders and consider the relative persuasiveness of the source, since certain authors and journals are considered more authoritative than others. The second place where one can find evidence of an international consensus regarding the standards applicable to arbitrator conduct is in published professional guidelines. There are three that are particularly important: the International Bar Association's Guidelines on Conflicts of Interest in International Arbitration, the International Bar Association's Rules of Ethics for International Arbitrators, and the American Arbitration Association's Code of Ethics for Arbitrators in Commercial Disputes. While US arbitrators and practitioners may be most familiar with the third of these guidelines, it is the IBA Guidelines that have become the most important. Much more detailed than the other two resources, the IBA Guidelines contain a groundbreaking hierarchy of relationships that are considered problematic ('red list' or 'waivable red list'), potentially problematic ('orange list'), or not problematic ('green list'). The IBA Guidelines also contain general principles to be used in situations not discussed in the specific lists. Whenever a challenge to an arbitrator arises, one should refer to these documents, even if they have not been officially adopted as binding in the arbitration agreement. Since all were drafted by working groups of international experts, they reflect what many consider to be 'best practices' in the field.

3.59 Third, advocates must be careful not to overlook the arbitration agreement itself, since it may place restrictions on who may serve as an arbitrator. For example, an arbitration agreement might indicate that the arbitrator may or may not be of a certain nationality, or state that the arbitrator is to be neutral as well as independent and impartial.

---

[46] Of course, states reserve to themselves the ability to prohibit any procedure that violates principles of mandatory law, such as basic due process. Therefore, if the challenge to the arbitrator implicates a fundamental principle of law, the national court will look to judicial principles of fairness and justice to help decide the issue.

(4) Researching recognition, enforcement, and challenge of an award

Once an award has been issued, parties have a choice on how to proceed. Those **3.60**
who have prevailed on the merits must decide whether they need to register or
confirm the award in the place where it was rendered, something that may not
be necessary as a matter of international practice but may be required under
domestic law to preserve the prevailing party's rights.[47] If the losing party does
not pay the award immediately, the prevailing party will need to bring judicial
proceedings to enforce the award.

The losing party also has options, both affirmative and defensive. Affirmatively, **3.61**
the loser can make a motion to set aside (vacate) or suspend the award, either
in the place where the award was rendered or in another court of competent
jurisdiction. Defensively, the losing party can object to the recognition or enforcement of the award. The grounds upon which the losing party may resist an award
may vary according to the procedural posture; for example, a party seeking to set
aside an award may have more grounds for doing so than would be the case if the
party were objecting to its enforcement internationally.[48]

Research in this area of law is relatively straightforward, since it is highly amenable **3.62**
to traditional research methodology. Because motions to set aside or enforce arbitral awards are always brought in the courts, there will be a great deal of statutory
and case law available concerning the relevant standards. Although international
legal instruments such as treaties and conventions provide the framework for
international enforcement, the bulk of the relevant law is found in national arbitration statutes and judicial opinions. Treatises and legal commentary are helpful
to the extent that gaps exist or policy rationales need to be fleshed out. Comparative
legal research regarding how other jurisdictions handle matters of trans-border
importance can also prove useful, particularly in instances where national law has
not been fully developed.

Once one has an understanding of what the relevant authorities are and where **3.63**
they can be found, one still must learn how to use them properly. The next chapter
discusses how experts in international commercial arbitration use the research
materials they have found.

---

[47] See eg, Lew et al (n 8), para 26-102.
[48] See eg, ibid, paras 25-31 to 25-50, 26-7 to 26-55.

4

HOW TO USE YOUR RESEARCH

A. Introduction

Previous chapters have described the type of legal authorities that exist in inter- **4.01** national arbitration, how those authorities are used by experienced advocates, what weight is given to those authorities by experienced arbitrators, and how to locate and use those authorities. This, however, is not enough. Both arbitrators and advocates still need to understand how research materials can and should be used in an international—as opposed to a domestic—arbitral proceeding. An advocate's failure to conform to at least some of the unwritten customs of international practice could lead him or her to alienate the arbitrator or otherwise diminish his or her credibility, while an arbitrator's failure to recognize the wide variety of legitimate ways of presenting information could cause him or her to make unwarranted judgments about the substance of the dispute when in fact the issue is only one of form.

Entire books have been written on the subject of advocacy in international com- **4.02** mercial arbitration, and those who wish a more detailed discussion of the subject should refer to those texts.[1] However, much of what is contained in those texts refers to oral advocacy or strategic issues, which are beyond the scope of the

---

[1] See eg, R Doak Bishop (ed), *The Art of Advocacy in International Arbitration* (Juris Publishing 2004); C Mark Baker, 'Advocacy in International Arbitration', in Lawrence Newman and Richard Hill (eds), *The Leading Arbitrators' Guide to International Arbitration* (Juris Publishing, 2008); 'Act I: Case Strategy and Written Advocacy', 21 Arbitration International 541 (2005).

current discussion. Surprisingly little is said about written advocacy. Therefore, this chapter will address three research-related issues, including:

- adapting the form of written pleadings and memoranda of law to take into account the perspective of one's arbitrator or opponents;
- citing supporting authority; and
- submitting written testimony from expert witnesses.

B. Adapting Written Pleadings and Memoranda of Law

4.03 Because there is no single, overarching adjudicating authority in international commercial arbitration, there is no single 'right' way to draft pleadings and papers, despite the fact that these documents carry a great deal of weight in international proceedings.[2] Furthermore, little is said in most arbitral rules about what written submissions can or should be made or what form those submissions should take.[3] This custom makes sense, at least on one level, because arbitration was intended to do away with excess formality and legalism. Under these circumstances, the creation or promotion of a single form of written submissions would be inappropriate.

4.04 Thus, advocates must rely on their experience, judgment, and discretion to identify the best manner of presenting written submissions to an arbitrator. Unfortunately, those who have not had a great deal of experience in international arbitration sometimes do not realize that what constitutes a best practice in a domestic court or domestic arbitration does not necessarily translate to a best practice in international arbitration. Furthermore, what is optimal in one international proceeding may not work in all proceedings. Therefore advocates need to

---

[2] See eg, Hans Smit, 'Managing an International Arbitration: An Arbitrator's View', 5 The American Review of International Arbitration 129 (1994). Smit writes that pleadings 'must contain not only all allegations of material facts, but also all arguments of law and all evidence upon which reliance is placed, and must be accompanied by written statements of all witnesses and copies of all documentary evidence relied on'. Ibid at 132. The need for comprehensive written submissions is based on the fact that '[a]t the hearing, witnesses, if heard at all, are examined only on cross-examination and rebuttal'. Ibid at 133. Although this is a somewhat conservative view, it is better to prepare written submissions as comprehensively as possible, on the off-chance that oral testimony may be curtailed.

[3] Rule sets do describe the basic requirements for demanding arbitration and setting forth the affirmative and defensive case, as well as contemplating the possibility of other sorts of written submissions, but give no guidance regarding length, style, or formatting. Some guidance is provided in a series of articles published in 2005 by Arbitration International concerning advocacy in international arbitration, particularly in 'Act I: Case Strategy and Written Advocacy', 21 Arbitration International 541 (2005). Individual arbitral institutions may also provide guidance for those proceeding under their rule sets. See eg, *Report from the ICC Commission on Arbitration, Techniques for Controlling Time and Costs in Arbitration* (ICC Publishing, 2007) paras 45–51.

be prepared to adapt themselves to the circumstances that arise in the arbitration at hand rather than automatically adopting approaches used in litigation or trying to create their own boilerplate approach to international commercial disputes.

Although the need to adapt submissions may be highest when the arbitrators, **4.05** advocates, and parties come from different legal traditions, care must be taken even when everyone comes from the same general legal tradition (common law, civil law, Islamic law). National differences still exist within a particular legal tradition. For example, legal practices in the United States differ significantly from those in the United Kingdom, despite the fact that both are technically common law countries. The same is true of civil law and Islamic nations—categorization of a jurisdiction as falling within the 'civil law' or 'Islamic' tradition allows for only gross generalizations about procedural preferences.

Taking other nations' or legal systems' approaches into account does not require **4.06** a lawyer to disregard his or her training and emulate another legal approach completely. What it does mean is that advocates and arbitrators should be prepared to: (a) understand and recognize that other lawyers may do things differently, and (b) shift towards the middle ground between the two (or more) relevant traditions. Insisting that one's own way is the best or only way seldom yields positive results, particularly when representing a client. After all, persuasion is an advocate's main goal, not adherence to a particular way of doing things. Similarly, an arbitrator's task is to see past the form of a submission and weigh the substantive merits of competing legal arguments.

A simple example demonstrates how much written submissions can vary within **4.07** a single legal tradition. At one end of the common law spectrum is American-style advocacy. American attorneys put a high premium on emotional appeal in their pleadings and learn to tell a story with strong personal connections, even if the dispute involves highly technical arguments between two commercial entities. Often, the facts are intentionally presented in a manner that lawyers trained in other traditions may perceive as inflammatory or biased. Furthermore, American lawyers commonly include multiple causes of action as part of a single complaint. It is unusual to see a single legal claim asserted (three to five seem to be a more typical number in a relatively simple case), and some particularly complex disputes could include allegations of twenty or more different causes of action as part of a single complaint. Furthermore, American-trained lawyers often take the approach that 'more is more' (as opposed to 'less is more') and file voluminous submissions if not given a page limit.[4] While this is not always

---

4 Recently, an American lawyer in Washington State filed a complaint that was 465 pages long. In that case, the US District Court judge ordered the lawyer to shorten the submission, using little-seen judicial humour. The court order read: 'Plaintiff has a great deal to say,/ But it seems he skipped

the case—US lawyers can be quite succinct when necessary[5]—many believe that American pleadings and submission are longer than those found in other jurisdictions.[6] Therefore, lawyers and arbitrators from outside the US should be prepared for this style of advocacy when one of the parties is represented by a US lawyer.[7]

4.08 Advocacy in England, on the other hand, tends to be more formal and succinct, in terms of both the pleadings and memorials. Pleadings tend to be quite brief, incorporating a 'letter before action' in addition to a short, formulaic claim. Rather than submitting lengthy pre-trial legal submissions, for example, as is done in the US, English barristers offer short 'skeleton arguments' that comprise a bare bones outline of what will be presented in court.[8] The language contains fewer emotive appeals, and although advocates still 'tell a story', that story tends to be more legal in nature than the type told in the US, as perhaps befits a legal system that has abolished the use of juries in all civil cases except those involving defamation. Those who have not practised in the United Kingdom or in matters involving British lawyers may be surprised by the brevity and objectivity of such submissions. However, one should never underestimate the persuasiveness of the British style of advocacy, which stands as a model for many lawyers trained in British Commonwealth and former Commonwealth nations. Civil law lawyers, particularly those from European nations, also look on this type of advocacy with approval.

4.09 Just as there can be no overarching generalizations about written submissions from common law jurisdictions, there is no 'standard' form of submissions used in civil law nations. Still, some observations can be made. For example, because

---

Rule 8(a)./ His Complaint is too long,/ Which renders it wrong,/ Please re-write and re-file today'. See <http://seattletimes.nwsource.com/html/localnews/2008033157_funnyjudge04m.html>.

[5] The lawyer mentioned in the preceding footnote was able to argue a different motion successfully using only a two-page submission. Ibid.

[6] This position is not universal. One commentator claims that American pleadings are short and only contain enough detail to put the defendant on notice of the allegations being brought. R Doak Bishop, 'Toward an Harmonized Approach to Advocacy in International Arbitration', in Bishop (n 1), 451, 468–9. It may be that the commentator was distinguishing between pleadings and other submissions. However, it is the author's experience that both pleadings and memoranda of law are much longer in the United States than elsewhere, since US lawyers view every written submission as an opportunity to influence the decision-maker.

[7] Examples of US-style advocacy in the US federal courts can be found online at <http://www.pacer.uscourts.gov>. Documents may be downloaded for a minimal charge.

[8] English court documents were not publicly available until very recently. Unlike the US, which allows for electronic public access to many cases, English submissions must be requested in writing. However, copies of skeleton arguments and other legal filings can now be found online. For example, see <http://www.peacetaxseven.com/skeleton.html> for examples of different types of papers submitted in the English Court of Appeal, including skeleton arguments. An example of a skeleton argument from a different case can be found at <http://www.bna.com/bnabooks/ababna/annual/2000/mcmullen.pdf>.

civil law cases are often decided primarily 'on the papers' (as opposed to after an adversarial trial),[9] pleadings can be quite lengthy, including both factual and legal allegations. On the other hand, some civil law practitioners submit shorter initial pleadings, waiting until after any hearings and rulings on evidence before fleshing out their arguments. Civil law lawyers may or may not separate their discussion of the facts from their discussion of the law in the same way that common law lawyers do. Furthermore, there can be differences in the way common law lawyers and civil law lawyers develop their legal arguments, with civil law lawyers often seeming to focus more heavily than common law lawyers do on public policies underlying the legal rules.[10] Conversely, common law lawyers are said to spend more time developing the facts than civil law lawyers do.[11]

Given these differences in approach, good internationalists try to present their legal and factual arguments in a manner that will resonate with the arbitrator. Although substance should always prevail over form, making a good first impression often relies on a writer's ability to conform to the reader's unstated (and often unconscious) expectations. Therefore, when preparing to draft any submissions in an international commercial arbitration, lawyers should locate: (a) models of pleadings and memorials of the type used in the national courts of both the arbitrator and opposing counsel, to better understand the expectations and predilections of lawyers who practise in those jurisdictions, as well as (b) models of submissions used in international commercial arbitration, preferably under the arbitral rules applicable to the dispute at hand (if any), to better understand how national norms are adapted for use in international proceedings.[12] As always, advocates should try to ensure that they are using models that illustrate the 'best practices' in the field. While it is possible that even the best lawyers from the most prestigious firms can produce poor papers on occasion, those who are new to the field would likely be best served by looking at publicly available samples from well-known practitioners, at least until they can develop a comprehensive file containing their own precedents.

4.10

---

9 However, some civil law systems use an 'adversarial', rather than 'inquisitorial', system, contrary to many generalizations about the differences between common law and civil law proceedings. See eg, Kaj Hobér, 'Advocacy in International Commercial Arbitration: Sweden', in Bishop (n 1), 169, 175.

10 Bishop (n 1), 455.

11 Bishop (n 1), 454.

12 Court documents are becoming more readily available online, either through the courts themselves (see eg, <http://www.pacer.uscourts.gov>) or through private actors (see eg, <http://www.peacetaxseven.com/skeleton.html>). Submissions in international class arbitration (a specialized form of commercial arbitration) may be found on the American Arbitration Association website (see <http://www.adr.org/sp.asp?id=25562>) and blank form precedents are published in certain specialized arbitral resources (see John Tackaberry and Arthur Marriott, *Bernstein's Handbook on Arbitration and Dispute Resolution Practice* (Sweet & Maxwell, 2003)). As always, lawyers must use their own best judgment to determine whether the precedent used is a worthy one and suitable to their particular dispute.

C. Citing Supporting Authority

4.11 Lawyers establish the credibility of their research in two ways. First, they present their arguments as a cohesive and persuasive whole, structuring the facts and legal theories in a way that leads the arbitrator to the inexorable conclusion that their client must prevail. Every advocate is well aware of the kinds of strategic decisions that must be made when preparing written submissions, but those who are involved in an international commercial arbitration must also take into account the special considerations associated with trans-national legal practice. Those types of global issues have been discussed in the previous section. This section discusses the second consideration: how to present the component elements of one's legal research—ie, the individual legal authorities—in a credible and persuasive manner.

4.12 Every legal system weighs different types of legal authority differently, and a good internationalist takes the predispositions of the arbitrator and other advocates into account when conducting legal research. As a matter of substance, a good practitioner offers support for each proposition of law from a variety of sources so that the arbitrator feels confident that the suggested outcome is correct. However, the impact of legal authority can be diminished if the material is not well presented as a matter of style. Therefore, wise advocates are careful to present their legal research in such a way that none of it goes to waste.

4.13 First, every proposition of law needs supporting authority, whether that authority is found in a statute, judicial opinion, arbitral rule, or legal commentary. In many jurisdictions, one reference per concept is enough—there is no reason to belabour the point by identifying numerous sources that provide the same result unless the intent is to show universal and multi-jurisdictional support for that particular idea. Though the practice of providing multiple authorities for a particular proposition of law is becoming outmoded in the United States, some US-trained lawyers still follow the practice of 'string citing' several (often minor or only tangentially relevant) cases to demonstrate widespread acceptance of a particular holding. Cutting down on this practice will go a long way towards demonstrating to an arbitrator that the lawyer in question is a knowledgeable specialist in international arbitration.

4.14 Second, there are regional differences relating to how often one references the same source. In the United States, lawyers are trained to use 'pinpoint cites' to reference the precise page that supports each proposition of law. It is not unusual for every sentence in a paragraph to contain a reference, even if it is to the same source.[13] As a result, any discussion of law authored by an American lawyer is

---

[13] American-trained lawyers use a variety of methods to shorten the length of the citations, including the widespread use of 'id' (which is an abbreviation for 'ibid', meaning the source that

littered either with footnotes or citations embedded within the body of the text. To a US-trained jurist, this appears neither presumptuous nor pedantic—instead, it properly differentiates between what is being put forward as law versus what is being put forward as argument or opinion. However, those who practise outside the United States do not view American citing conventions in the same light.

Lawyers trained outside the United States use a much lighter hand when refer- **4.15** encing legal authority in their written submissions. The legal analysis is not any less detailed or rigorous than that of American colleagues—the common practice in other countries simply is to cite legal resources only when absolutely necessary. If the reference is clear from the context of the discussion, there is no need to include a citation at the end of every sentence. Citations to particular pages are typically only necessary when the author has included quoted material or if the author has interspersed material from other sources or the author's own opinion.[14] Therefore, a source may appear only once in a discussion, either at the beginning or the end of a paragraph or section. Advocates and arbitrators should be aware of the difference in citation style, so as to avoid making snap judgments about the weight to be given a written submission based only on the number of explicit references to legal authorities. If the author's meaning is clear and the analysis cogent, it should not matter whether there are many or few footnotes. Of course, those who are aware of the way that different jurisdictions view the question of citations will be able to adapt their drafting style so as not to test the understanding or patience of their readers.

Third, practitioners need to consider the form of the citation. There are numer- **4.16** ous guides to how legal materials should be referenced, but all of them have the same goal in mind: helping the drafter identify different authorities with enough specificity so that a curious reader can find the item independently. In the United States, the standard text describing how to cite legal authorities is *The Bluebook: A Uniform System of Citation*, published by the Harvard Law Review Association. The United Kingdom has several similar texts, though one could also simply refer to *The Oxford Standard for Citation of Legal Authorities*, which is available online and is typically considered the most authoritative reference of its kind.[15] Other countries have their own similar reference authorities, and advocates in

---

comes immediately before) or 'id at [page number]'. US lawyers also use the phrase 'supra note [number]' to refer to previously cited secondary material.

[14] Even though lawyers trained outside the US use fewer citations, they still use abbreviations and short citation forms to make reading easier. Two common short-form references used in the United Kingdom are 'ibid' to refer to material immediately preceding the reference and 'op cit', or 'from the work cited', to refer to material previously cited in the section or chapter.

[15] See <http://denning.law.ox.ac.uk/published/oscola.shtml>.

international arbitration can refer to any one of these for assistance.[16] Sometimes it's best to find out how an authority is cited in its home jurisdiction and replicate that form in the submissions to the arbitrator, though that can be tricky in situations where there are many different source references of which only one is considered the 'official' source.[17] Although it can be helpful to an arbitrator to see a legal citation in a familiar form, it is more important for the drafter to include all the necessary information to find the source in the reference. Consistency within the document itself is of course expected as well.

4.17 Fourth and finally, sometimes a reference is not enough. Some legal authorities appear in sources that are not easily accessible, no matter how well-written the form of the citation. In those instances, advocates should include a proper reference to the materials in the text of the submission, but should also attach a copy of the statute, decision, or excerpted material in an appendix. The goal is to make the arbitrator's job easier, not harder, and requiring him or her to search for a difficult-to-locate source is neither good practice (since it will not endear you to the arbitrator) nor good business (since most arbitrators charge by the hour). Furthermore, if it is necessary to translate an authority into the language of the arbitration, the lawyers should include both the original source and the text of the source in translation. Producing a certified translation by an independent agent is often best, even if it is expensive, as it protects the lawyers (and their clients) from any allegation of wrongdoing if any errors creep into the process.

D. Submitting Testimony from Expert Witnesses

4.18 International commercial arbitration often involves complex issues of law and facts, and arbitrators may benefit from expert testimony on issues involving scientific or technical matters, economic trends, accounting procedures, and even questions of national law. Expert testimony can prove useful in determining one or all of these issues. However, there appears to be a great deal of variation in the frequency with which expert testimony is offered, with some lawyers—typically those trained in the United States—being accused of overusing expert testimony while others—typically those from outside the US—being said to underuse it.[18]

---

[16] However, most reference books like *The Bluebook* and *The Oxford Standard for Citation of Legal Authorities* indicate how a practitioner is to cite authorities from other nations, so one does not need to go to many different reference books to find out how to cite materials from foreign jurisdictions.

[17] Judicial opinions in both the United States and England are published in numerous reports, but only one is considered the 'official' reporting series (and that determination may depend on which court one is in). At one time, lawyers in the US referenced all possible locations (both official and unofficial) where a source was published, but that practice is on the decline as courts impose stricter page limits on submissions.

[18] Bishop (n 1), 464.

The general rule regarding use of expert testimony in US courts is reflected in the **4.19**
Federal Rules of Evidence,[19] Rule 702, which reads:

> If scientific, technical, or other specialized knowledge will assist the trier of fact to
> understand the evidence or to determine a fact in issue, a witness qualified as an
> expert by knowledge, skill, experience, training, or education, may testify thereto in
> the form of an opinion or otherwise, if (1) the testimony is based upon sufficient
> facts or data, (2) the testimony is the product of reliable principles and methods,
> and (3) the witness has applied the principles and methods reliably to the facts of
> the case.

Experts may even testify on 'ultimate issues' (ie, issues which are determinative of **4.20**
the case).[20] However, there are some guidelines regarding the material which is
used by an expert in coming to his or her conclusion. Rule 703 states:

> The facts or data in the particular case upon which an expert bases an opinion or
> inference may be those perceived by or made known to the expert at or before the
> hearing. If of a type reasonably relied upon by experts in the particular field in
> forming opinions or inferences upon the subject, the facts or data need not be
> admissible in evidence in order for the opinion or inference to be admitted. Facts or
> data that are otherwise inadmissible shall not be disclosed to the jury by the propo-
> nent of the opinion or inference unless the court determines that their probative
> value in assisting the jury to evaluate the expert's opinion substantially outweighs
> their prejudicial effect.

Furthermore, experts may be required to disclose the facts upon which their
testimony is based under US procedural law.[21]

Given this approach, it is no wonder that American lawyers not only use expert **4.21**
testimony freely, but provide large amounts of supporting documentation and
factual discussion along with that testimony.[22] In some cases, the expert submissions may even be longer in arbitration than in litigation, since: (a) written submissions in arbitration may, in some cases, replace affirmative oral testimony
(and thus are drafted to be more comprehensive than a simple expert report), and
(b) written submissions in arbitration typically attach the documentary evidence
on which the testimony relies.[23]

---

[19] Although the Federal Rules of Evidence are only applicable to US federal courts, many state
courts use similar rules regarding the introduction and use of evidence.

[20] US Federal Rules of Evidence, Rule 704.

[21] Ibid, Rule 705.

[22] The excessive use of expert testimony in the US has been limited somewhat by the US Supreme
Court decisions in *Daubert v Merrell Dow Pharmaceuticals*, 509 US 579 (1993), and *Kumho Tire
Co v Carmichael*, 526 US 137 (1999).

[23] In US litigation, documentary evidence must be properly entered into evidence at trial in
accordance with the applicable rules of evidence, rather than simply submitted for consideration, as
is the case in arbitration.

4.22 Although US-trained lawyers may see great benefit in using expert reports and testimony, they would be well-advised to keep such submissions to a reasonable length so as not to put off the arbitrator in international proceedings. Conversely, lawyers from other jurisdictions may want to consider expanding their expert testimony so as to take full advantage of this particularly useful evidentiary device. In all instances, advocates should be aware that many arbitral rules permit the arbitrator to appoint a neutral expert, which could minimize the type of 'battle of the experts' that jurists in many countries find alarming.

4.23 Again, questions will arise as to the form of the expert's written submission. Since experts deal with highly technical or complex matters, the focus should be on educating the arbitrator in a simple but non-condescending manner, remembering that it is always more persuasive to show how an expert reached a particular conclusion rather than simply stating the conclusion itself. Whatever form fulfils that purpose best should be appropriate, and the formats used may vary according to the discipline in which the expert works. For example, some expert testimony may make the most sense when illustrated graphically, whereas others can be portrayed best through words or photographs. Some creativity is allowed when presenting expert testimony.

4.24 The discussion in this and earlier chapters provides general guidance in how to conduct research in international commercial arbitration as well as how to present that evidence. The following section will help lawyers locate the sources used most often in this specialized field of law.

5

LEGAL AUTHORITIES IN INTERNATIONAL COMMERCIAL ARBITRATION— BIBLIOGRAPHIC SOURCES

A. Introduction

Chapters 1–4 of this book discussed how to identify the types of legal authorities **5.01** that are relevant to international commercial arbitration as well as how to use those resources. This chapter describes where researchers can find some of the most often used materials in this specialized field of law. Roughly speaking, there are eight categories of legal authority to consider:

- conventions and treaties;
- national laws;
- arbitral rules;
- law of the dispute (procedural orders and agreements between the parties);
- arbitral awards;
- case law;

- treatises and monographs; and
- legal articles.

5.02 A list of available resources in each of the eight categories is included below. The lists contain information on both traditional print resources as well as electronic resources.[1] However, space limitations require the following to be more of a practical guide than a comprehensive one, so the entries concentrate primarily on leading and current resources available in English.[2] Before describing materials in the eight categories, a short discussion of electronic resources is in order.

B. Specialized Electronic Databases

5.03 The rapid rise of computerized legal research, as well as the advent of institutionally and individually maintained websites, has revolutionized how researchers approach questions in international commercial arbitration. Some practitioners choose to begin their research in general legal databases that are available to them via subscription services, whereas other lawyers choose to start their investigations by accessing free websites maintained by individuals or institutions interested in international arbitration. Those with a subscription to a commercial database specializing in arbitration may focus their early efforts there. However, each of these databases is different, and experienced practitioners expand their searches beyond any single source and make sure to consult a variety of print and electronic sources to verify and supplement their preliminary findings.

(1) Free online services

5.04 Perhaps the easiest and certainly the least expensive means of conducting electronic research is through free websites maintained by arbitral institutions, non-profit organizations, law schools, and individuals interested in international commercial arbitration. These websites can include the text of relevant treaties, conventions,

---

[1] Website addresses are live at the time this book goes to press. However, internet addresses can change at any time, and there is no way to ensure that the addresses will still be in operation at any future date. Furthermore, not everything that is published on the internet is accurate. Readers should always consider the reliability of the source of any electronic information and should take any steps that are necessary to ensure that the information that they use is correct and up to date.

[2] The most comprehensive and multi-lingual bibliography in this area of law is Hans Smit et al, The Pechota Bibliography on Arbitration (JurisNet LLC, loose-leaf). Already over 1,200 pages in length, The Pechota Bibliography is a loose-leaf service and continues to grow with the publication of every new article and book on arbitration in every language. Annual bibliographies are also available in Albert Jan van den Berg (ed), Yearbook Commercial Arbitration (Kluwer Law International, annual). Online bibliographies are maintained by the Centre for Transnational Law ('CENTRAL'), found at <http://www.tldb.net/>, and by the United Nations Commission on International Trade Law ('UNCITRAL'), found at <http://www.uncitral.org/uncitral/en/publications/bibliography.html>.

national laws, judicial opinions, arbitral rules, arbitral awards and/or expert commentary, as well as links to other potentially relevant websites. Although the websites are not all maintained with the same degree of frequency, they can provide a good introduction to the sources and concepts used in international commercial arbitration.

Each site's focus and content are different, so researchers may need to consult **5.05** several before finding the necessary information. There are too many sites to list individually, but a useful start can be made at the following locations:

American Arbitration Association ('AAA') Centre for International Dispute Resolution ('ICDR')—<http://www.adr.org/sp.asp?id=28819>

American Society of International Law ('ASIL') Guide to Electronic Resources for International Law (international commercial arbitration section)—<http://www.asil.org/arb1.cfm>

CENTRAL Transnational Law Digest & Bibliography—<http://www.tldb.net>

Electronic Information System for International Law ('EISIL')—<http://www.eisil.org/index.php?sid=663105939&t=sub_pages&cat=790>

International Chamber of Commerce ('ICC') International Court of Arbitration—<http://www.iccwbo.org/policy/arbitration/id2882/index.html>

International Commercial Arbitration: Locating the Sources, on LLRX.com, maintained by Jean M Wenger, Documents/Foreign and International Law Librarian, Cook County Law Library, Chicago, Illinois, USA—<http://www.llrx.com/features/arbitration2.htm>

International Commercial Arbitration: Resources in Print and Electronic Format, maintained by Lyonette Louis-Jacques, Foreign and International Law Librarian and Lecturer in Law, University of Chicago Law School, USA—<http://www2.lib.uchicago.edu/~llou/intlarb.html>

Lex Mercatoria: International Commercial Arbitration, hosted by the Law Faculty of the University of Oslo, Norway—<http://www.jus.uio.no/lm/arbitration/toc.html>

London Court of International Arbitration ('LCIA')—<http://www.lcia-arbitration.com>

Permanent Court of Arbitration at The Hague—<http://www.pca-cpa.org>

TMC Asser Institute for Private and Public International Law—<http://www.asser.nl/ica/index.htm>

United Nations Commission on International Trade Law ('UNCITRAL')—<http://www.uncitral.org/uncitral/en/index.html>

United Nations Conference on International Trade and Development, International Investment Agreements[3]—<http://www.unctad.org/Templates/StartPage.asp?intItemID=2310&lang=1>

(2) Subscription services

5.06 Although free online websites can be helpful as an introductory matter, most serious legal research is done through traditional print sources and specialized online or electronic subscription services. The subscription services are often associated with different publishing houses, and as such, tend to reflect the materials that are contained in that publisher's print catalogue. Therefore, a comparison of the different subscription services tends to be 'apples to oranges', and researchers will seldom find a service that meets all of their needs. Those who work routinely in the field of international commercial arbitration will likely need to sign up with several different online providers or fill the gaps in their online service with print copies of other references.

5.07 The contents of each subscription service change somewhat regularly as international arbitration grows in popularity and yields more dedicated resources, and as international publishing houses merge and consolidate. Those who are interested in purchasing a subscription should check the contents of similar resources before deciding on one, since every service will vary in what it offers and some materials may be more valuable than others to the purchaser. Electronic databases can typically be accessed either through CD-ROM or via a password-protected website.

5.08 There are two types of electronic services available by subscription: (1) general legal databases that include some arbitration materials and (2) specialized databases that focus only (or primarily) on international commercial arbitration. At this time, there are two subscription databases specializing in international arbitration. They are:

Arbitration Law online—<http://www.arbitrationlaw.com/online>

Kluwer Arbitration online[4]—<http://www.kluwerarbitration.com>

Two other subscription databases focus on a wider selection of public and private international law issues, including, but not limited to, arbitration. They are:

The Hague Academy Collected Courses Online/Recueil des cours de l'Académie de la Haye en ligne, available through Martinus Nijhoff Publishers—<http://www.brill.nl/haco>

---

[3] The United Nations has issued a compendium of international investment instruments, including those that are multilateral, regional, and bilateral in nature, as well as those involving non-governmental organizations. The compendia may be accessed online at <http://www.unctad.org/Templates/Page.asp?intItemID=2323&lang=1>.

[4] In addition to its internet service, Kluwer Law International also offers a CD-ROM entitled 'Resources on International Commercial Arbitration'.

Transnational Dispute Management—<http://www.transnational-dispute-management.com/>

Finally, there are general legal databases that provide legal information on a wide **5.09** range of subjects. Although these databases contain information relevant to international commercial arbitration, they do not tend to include the specialized legal resources that make international commercial arbitration unique. Nevertheless, general legal databases contain some important information that usually isn't found on the specialized databases. For example, the general sources often have access to a much wider range of non-specialist legal journals, which can be valuable since these journals often contain useful articles on international arbitration. General databases may also have a wider or deeper range of statutory and judicial materials from foreign jurisdictions. Some of the more widely available general legal databases include:

Hein Online—<http://heinonline.org>

Informa—<http://www.i-law.com>

LegalTrac[5]—<http://www.gale.cengage.com/servlet/ItemDetailServlet?region=9&imprint=000&titleCode=INFO31&type=4&id=172054>

LexisNexis—<http://www.lexisnexis.com>

Practical Law Company—<http://www.practicallaw.com>

Westlaw—<http://www.westlaw.com>

C. Conventions and Treaties

Conventions and treaties are signed by states, but bind private actors (and some **5.10** public actors) to the terms of those agreements through domestic application of the treaty provisions. These international instruments may be bilateral or multilateral in nature. Because of space limitations, this section focuses only on the most common multilateral agreements concerning arbitration.[6]

International instruments typically appear in a variety of different print locations. **5.11** Some of these sources are considered 'official' (and thus constitute the legally

---

[5] The information on LegalTrac (which is not to be confused with Legal Trac) is accessible in electronic form as a CD-ROM and in traditional print form as the *Current Law Index*. It can also be accessed online through both Westlaw and LexisNexis under the name 'Legal Resources Index'.

[6] A list of bilateral investment treaties can be found at <http://icsid.worldbank.org/ICSID/FrontServlet?requestType=ICSIDPublicationsRH&actionVal=ViewBilateral&reqFrom=Main>. The United Nations has also published an online list of bilateral investment treaties that is current through 1999. See <http://www.unctad.org/en/docs/poiteiiad2.en.pdf>.

binding version of that instrument) and others are not.[7] Furthermore, many international instruments can also be found online, again either through 'official' websites sponsored by the international organization(s) that promulgated the instrument or through websites that carry copies of the document. Researchers must be careful when dealing with any 'unofficial' source—be it in print or electronic—and confirm that the text of the document that they are using is correct and current.

5.12 It has become a tradition in international commercial arbitration for treatises to include the text of commonly used international agreements in the appendices. This practice dates back to the days before electronic research, when access to materials was more difficult. However, this custom can still provide researchers with helpful shortcuts, so long as the lawyers confirm that the version reproduced in the treatise is, in fact, the same as that found in 'official' sources.

5.13 Another practice that arose in the days before electronic research was the compilation of a wide variety of treaties and conventions relating to international commercial arbitration in a single sourcebook. Many of these compilation texts are published in loose-leaf form, which ensures their currency. Some useful series include:

> Bergsten, Eric E, International Commercial Arbitration (Oxford University Press, loose-leaf)
>
> Bergsten, Eric E, International Commercial Arbitration Pacific Rim (Oxford University Press, loose-leaf)
>
> Smit, Hans and Vratislav Pechota (eds), International Arbitration Treaties (Juris Publishing, 2005)
>
> Smit, Hans and Vratislav Pechota (eds), World Arbitration Reporter, Vol 1 (Juris Publishing, loose-leaf)

5.14 Treaties and conventions can also be found individually. Following is a list of some of the more common international instruments relating to commercial arbitration. Not all of these will apply to every proceeding. In fact, many lawyers will not ever need to become familiar with anything other than the United Nations Convention on the Recognition and Enforcement of Foreign Arbitral Awards ('New York Convention').[8] Nevertheless, parties should consider whether any of the following instruments apply to their dispute.

> 1899 Convention for the Pacific Settlement of International Disputes ('The Hague Convention')
> Print sources: July 29, 1899, 26 Martens NRG, 2d ser 920; 1 Bevans 230
> Online source: <http://www.pca-cpa.org/showpage.asp?pag_id=1037>

---

[7] For example, as a matter of US practice, International Legal Materials ('ILM') is not considered an 'official' source for any international treaty to which the United States is a party.

[8] June 10, 1958, 330 UNTS 3, TIAS No 6997.

1907 Convention for the Pacific Settlement of International Disputes
('The Hague Convention')
Print sources: Oct 18, 1907, 3 Martens NRG 3d ser 360; 205 CTS 233
Online source: <http://www.pca-cpa.org/showpage.asp?pag_id=1037>

1923 Geneva Protocol on Arbitration Clauses ('Geneva Protocol')
Print source: Sept 24, 1923, 27 LNTS 157
Online source: <http://www.jurisint.org/doc/html/ins/en/2002/
2002jiinsen5.html>

1927 Geneva Convention on the Execution of Foreign Awards ('Geneva
Convention')
Print source: Sept 26, 1927, 92 LNTS 301
Online source: <http://www.jurisint.org/doc/html/ins/en/2000/
2000jiinsen68.html>

1958 United Nations Convention on the Recognition and Enforcement of
Foreign Arbitral Awards ('New York Convention')
Print sources: June 10, 1958, 330 UNTS 3, TIAS No 6997
Online source: <http://www.uncitral.org/uncitral/en/uncitral_texts/
arbitration/NYConvention.html>

1961 European Convention on International Commercial Arbitration
('Geneva Convention')
Print source: Apr 21, 1961, 484 UNTS 364
Online source: <http://www.jurisint.org/doc/html/ins/en/2002/
2002jiinsen6.html>

1962 Agreement Relating to Application of the European Convention on
International Commercial Arbitration ('Paris Agreement')
Print sources: Dec 17, 1962, 523 UNTS 93, CETS No 042
Online source: <http://conventions.coe.int/Treaty/EN/Treaties/Html/
042.htm>

1965 Convention on the Settlement of Investment Disputes between States
and Nationals of Other States ('ICSID Convention' or 'Washington
Convention')
Print sources: Mar 18, 1965, 575 UNTS 159, TIAS 6090
Online source: <http://icsid.worldbank.org/ICSID/Index.jsp>

1966 European Convention Providing a Uniform Law on Arbitration
('Strasbourg Arbitration Convention')
Print source: Jan 20, 1966, CETS No 56 (has not entered into force)
Online source: <http://conventions.coe.int/Treaty/Commun/
QueVoulezVous.asp?NT=056&CM=8&DF=2/19/05&CL=ENG>

1969 Vienna Convention on the Law of Treaties
Print source: May 23, 1969, 1155 UNTS 331
Online source: <http://untreaty.un.org/ilc/texts/instruments/english/conventions/1_1_1969.pdf>

1970 Hague Convention on the Taking of Evidence Abroad in Civil or Commercial Matters
Print source: July 27, 1970, 847 UNTS 231
Online source: <http://www.jus.uio.no/lm/hcpil.taking.of.evidence.abroad.in.civil.or.commercial.matters.convention.1971/doc.html>

1972 Convention on the Settlement of Civil Law Disputes Resulting from Economic, Scientific and Technological Co-operation ('Moscow Convention')
Print sources: May 26, 1972, 890 UNTS 167, translated in 13 ILM 5 (1972)
Online source: <http://www.jurisint.org/doc/html/ins/en/2000/2000jiinsen76.html>

1975 Inter-American Convention on International Commercial Arbitration ('Panama Convention')
Print sources: Jan 30, 1975, 1438 UNTS 245, 14 ILM 336
Online source: <http://www.sice.oas.org/dispute/comarb/iacac/iacac2e.asp>

1979 Inter-American Convention of Extraterritorial Validity of Foreign Judgments and Arbitral Awards ('Montevideo Convention')
Print source: May 8, 1979, 18 ILM 1224
Online source: <http://www.sice.oas.org/dispute/comarb/caicmoe.asp>

1980 Rome Convention on the Law Applicable to Contractual Obligations ('Rome Convention')
Print source: June 19, 1980, 1980 OJ (L 266) 1
Online source: <http://www.jus.uio.no/lm/ec.applicable.law.contracts.1980/doc.html>

1981 Declaration of the Government of the Democratic and Popular Republic of Algeria Concerning the Settlement of Claims by the Government of the United States of America and the Government of the Islamic Republic of Iran ('Algiers Declaration')
Print source: Jan 19, 1981, 20 ILM 230
Online source: <http://www.iusct.org/claims-settlement.pdf>

1982 UNCITRAL Recommendations to Assist Arbitral Institutions and Other Interested Bodies With Regard to Arbitrations Under the UNCITRAL Arbitration Rules

Print source: *UNCITRAL Yearbook Vol XIII*, pp 420–4 (1982)

Online source: <http://www.uncitral.org/uncitral/en/uncitral_texts/ arbitration/1982Recommendations_arbitration.html>

1985 Convention Establishing the Multilateral Investment Guarantee Agency ('MIGA')

Print sources: Oct 11, 1985, 1508 UNTS 99, 21 ILM 1605

Online source: <http://www.miga.org/quickref/index_sv.cfm?stid=1583>

1986 Agreement on Promotion, Protection and Guarantee of Investments Among Member States of the Organisation of the Islamic Conference ('OIC')

Print source: June 1–5, 1981, Doc Annex-I to ICFM[9] 1281-E/D.6

Online source: <http://www.unctad.org/en/docs/dtci30vol2_en.pdf>

1987 Amman Arab Convention on Commercial Arbitration

Print source: Apr 14, 1987, reprinted in *International Handbook on Commercial Arbitration Annex II-1* (Kluwer Law International, Jan 1990)

Online source: <http://www.jurisint.org/doc/html/ins/en/2000/ 2000jiinsen203.html>

1987 Agreement among the Government of Brunei Darussalam, the Republic of Indonesia, Malaysia, the Republic of the Philippines, the Republic of Singapore and the Kingdom of Thailand for the Promotion and Protection of Investments ('ASEAN')

Print source: Dec 15, 1987, 27 ILM 612

Online source: <http://www.aseansec.org/6464.htm>

1992 North American Free Trade Agreement ('NAFTA')

Print source: Dec 17, 1992, 32 ILM 605

Online source: <http://www.nafta-sec-alena.org/DefaultSite/index_e. aspx?DetailID=267>

1993 North American Agreement on Environmental Cooperation ('NAAEC')

Print source: Sept 13, 1993, 32 ILM 1480

Online source: <http://www.cec.org/pubs_info_resources/law_treat_ agree/naaec/index.cfm?varlan=english>

1993 Treaty Establishing the Organization for the Harmonization of Business Law in Africa ('OHADA')

Print source: Oct 7, 1993, Journal Officiel de l'OHADA 1 (Nov 1, 1997) (in French)

Online source: <http://www.jurisint.org/ohada/text/text.01.en.html>

---

9 'ICFM' refers to the Intergovernmental Council of Foreign Ministers of the Organisation of the Islamic Conference.

1994 Energy Charter Treaty
Print source: Dec 17, 1994, 34 ILM 360
Online source: <http://www.encharter.org/index.php?id=28>

1998 The MERCOSUR Agreement on International Commercial Arbitration[10]
Print source: July 23, 1998, MERCOSUR Council Dec No 3/98 (in Portuguese and Spanish)
Online source: <http://www.mercosur.int/msweb/portal% 20intermediario/es/index.htm> (in Portuguese and Spanish)

2006 Recommendation regarding interpretation of article II(2) and article VII(1) of the New York Convention
Print source: July 7, 2006, Report of the United Nations Commission on International Trade Law on the Work of its Thirty-Ninth Session, Supplement No 17, A/61/17 (June 19–July 7, 2006), at Annex II
Online source: <http://www.uncitral.org/pdf/english/texts/arbitration/ NY-conv/A2E.pdf>

D. National Laws

5.15 National laws on arbitration address a somewhat narrow range of issues, but are nevertheless very important to practitioners in this field. Although many states embrace their own unique statutory approach to arbitration, a growing number of jurisdictions have based their national laws on the United Nations Commission on International Trade Law's Model Law on International Commercial Arbitration ('UNCITRAL Model Law').[11] The UNICTRAL Model Law is not itself binding, but it has proven to be a homogenizing force in this area of law, since many states take the view that the provisions of the UNCITRAL Model Law should be interpreted in a similar manner throughout the world.

5.16 National laws may be found in the statute books in their place of origin or may be reprinted in other sources. For example, translated versions of arbitration statutes from states that are often used as arbitral seats may be found in translation online or in the appendices of some of the leading treatises on international arbitration.

---

[10] There is also an Agreement on International Commercial Arbitration signed between MERCOSUR, Bolivia, and Chile signed on the same date in 1998. See Mario JA Oyarzábal, 'Jurisdiction Over International Electronic Contracts: A View on Inter-American, MERCOSUR, and Argentine Rules', 19 Temple International and Comparative Law Journal 27 (2005).

[11] GA Res 40/72, 40 UN GAOR Supp (No 17), UN Doc A/40/17 (June 21, 1985). The UNCITRAL Model Law, which was adopted in 1985 with amendments in 2006, may also be found online at <http://www.uncitral.org/uncitral/en/uncitral_texts/arbitration/1985Model_arbitration. html> (original) and <http://www.uncitral.org/pdf/english/texts/arbitration/ml-arb/07-86998_ Ebook.pdf> (with amendments).

There are also a number of publications dedicated to translating and reproducing national statutes on arbitration, including the following:

Alford, Roger (ed), World Trade and Arbitration Materials (Kluwer Law International, periodical)

Bergsten, Eric E, International Commercial Arbitration (Oxford University Press, loose-leaf)

Bergsten, Eric E, International Commercial Arbitration Pacific Rim (Oxford University Press, loose-leaf)

Paulsson, Jan et al (eds), International Handbook on Commercial Arbitration: National Reports and Basic Legal Texts (Kluwer Law International, loose-leaf)[12]

Smit, Hans and Vratislav Pechota (eds), National Arbitration Laws (Juris Publishing, loose-leaf)

Smit, Hans and Vratislav Pechota (eds), World Arbitration Reporter, Vols II, IIA, and IIB (Juris Publishing, loose-leaf)

van den Berg, Albert Jan (ed), Yearbook Commercial Arbitration (Kluwer Law International, annual)[13]

Free online access to national arbitration statutes[14] can also be found at:

Asian Legal Information Institute—<http://www.asianlii.org/>

Australasian Legal Information Institute—<http://austlii.law.uts.edu.au/>

British and Irish Legal Information Institute—<http://www.bailii.org/>

Canadian Legal Information Institute—<http://www.canlii.org/>

Commonwealth Legal Information Institute—<http://www.commonlii.org/>

The Cyprus Source of Legal Information—<http://www.cylaw.org/index-en.html>

Hong Kong Legal Information Institute—<http://www.hklii.org/>

Irish Legal Information Initiative—<http://www.ucc.ie/law/irlii/index.php>

New Zealand Legal Information Initiative—<http://www.nzlii.org/>

---

[12] This publication is published through the cooperation of the International Council for International Arbitration ('ICCA') and has been edited at various times by both Albert Jan van den Berg and Pieter Sanders. The table of contents for the most recent supplement to the Handbook can be found at <http://www.arbitration-icca.org/publications.html>.

[13] The tables of contents for all of the Yearbooks (which were first published in 1976 and are put out by the International Council for Commercial Arbitration ('ICCA')) can be found at <http://www.arbitration-icca.org/publications/yearbook_table_of_contents.html>.

[14] Electronic access to national laws on arbitration may also be had through both the free and subscription services databases listed above under 'Specialized Electronic Databases'.

Pacific Islands Legal Information Initiative—<http://www.paclii.org/>

Southern African Legal Information Institute—<http://www.saflii.org/>

United Kingdom Territories and Dependencies Legal Information Initiative—
   <http://www.worldlii.org/catalog/3144.htm>l>

(United States) Legal Information Institute—<http://www.law.cornell.edu/>

World Legal Information Institute—<http://www.worldlii.org/>

E. Arbitral Rules

5.17 Most arbitral institutions publish their own set of arbitral rules which can then be adopted by interested parties.[15] The United Nations Commission on International Trade Law ('UNCITRAL')—which is not an arbitral institution in the same sense as the AAA, the ICC, or the LCIA—has also published a set of rules (the 'UNCITRAL Arbitration Rules')[16] which are frequently adopted by parties to arbitration.

5.18 Virtually all arbitral rules can now be found online at the institution's website, but there are many printed versions of the rules as well, typically in the appendices to leading treatises on arbitration or in volumes that compile a variety of arbitral materials. Some of the more useful texts include:

Alford, Roger (ed), World Trade and Arbitration Materials (Kluwer Law International, periodical)

Bergsten, Eric E, International Commercial Arbitration (Oxford University Press, loose-leaf)

Bergsten, Eric E, International Commercial Arbitration Pacific Rim (Oxford University Press, loose-leaf)

Simpson, Thacher & Bartlett LLP, *Comparison of Asian International Arbitration Rules* (Juris Publishing, 2003)

Simpson, Thacher & Bartlett LLP, *Comparison of International Arbitration Rules* (Juris Publishing, 2002)

Smit, Hans, *A Chart Comparing International Commercial Arbitration Rules* (Sweet & Maxwell, 1998)

---

[15] A comprehensive listing of national and international arbitral institutions is beyond the scope of this text, but a number of the more well-known organizations can be found in Paul J Davidson and Ludwik Kos-Racewicz-Zubkowski, *Commercial Arbitration Institutions: An International Directory and Guide* (Oceana Publications, 1992). A list of arbitral institutions is also published every year in Albert Jan van den Berg (ed), Yearbook Commercial Arbitration (Kluwer Law International, annual).

[16] GA Res 31/98, UN Doc A/RES/31/98 (Dec 15, 1976) also available at <http://www.uncitral.org/pdf/english/texts/arbitration/arb-rules/arb-rules.pdf>.

Smit, Hans and Vratislav Pechota (eds), Arbitration Rules—National Institutions (Juris Publishing, loose-leaf)

Smit, Hans and Vratislav Pechota (eds), Arbitration Rules—International Institutions (Juris Publishing, loose-leaf)

Smit, Hans and Vratislav Pechota (eds), World Arbitration Reporter, Vols III, IIA, IV, and IVB (Juris Publishing, loose-leaf)

van den Berg, Albert Jan (ed), Yearbook Commercial Arbitration (Kluwer Law International, annual)[17]

F. Law of the Dispute (Procedural Orders and Agreements Between the Parties)

The law of the dispute is particular to each arbitration and is not found in commercially published sources. Instead, parties need to look at formal and informal procedural orders issued by the arbitrator as well as agreements between the parties, including, but not limited to, the formal arbitration agreement. **5.19**

Although it can be difficult to change the law of the dispute once proceedings have begun (although amendments to arbitration agreements and procedural orders are, of course, entirely possible), the best time to try to shape the law of the dispute is when the arbitration agreement is still in the drafting stages. There are many ways that parties can individualize an arbitration agreement to ensure a procedure that suits their needs.[18] Those who need help in drafting an enforceable dispute resolution clause can find model language on the websites of the various arbitral institutions. Precedents are also available in treatises.[19] **5.20**

G. Arbitral Awards

Although arbitral awards are not binding on anyone other than the parties to that particular arbitration, published awards can provide persuasive guidance on a number of different subjects. Awards are particularly helpful when considering **5.21**

---

[17] The tables of contents for all of the Yearbooks (which were first published in 1976 and are put out by the International Council for Commercial Arbitration ('ICCA')) can be found at <http://www.arbitration-icca.org/publications/yearbook_table_of_contents.html>.

[18] See eg, Alan Redfern and Martin Hunter et al, *Law and Practice of International Commercial Arbitration* (Sweet & Maxwell, 2004) paras 8-20 to 8-73; Stephen R Bond, 'How to Draft an Arbitration Clause', 6 Journal of International Arbitration 65 (1989); Dr Iur Oliver Dillenz, 'Drafting International Commercial Arbitration Clauses', 21 Suffolk Transnational Law Review 221 (1998).

[19] See eg, John Tackaberry and Arthur Marriott, *Bernstein's Handbook on Arbitration and Dispute Resolution Practice, Vol 2* (Sweet & Maxwell, 2003).

issues that are not covered by national statutes and/or that are seldom discussed in national courts. Important areas of concern include procedural matters and challenges to arbitrators, but published awards can help with research on any number of topics.

5.22 Several major international arbitral institutions publish awards and decisions arising out of international commercial arbitrations to assist parties in anticipating how similar disputes might be resolved in the future. These awards and decisions are available in printed form, including both bound and loose-leaf editions, as well as in electronic form.

> Alford, Roger (ed), World Trade and Arbitration Materials (Kluwer Law International, periodical)
>
> ASA Bulletin (Wolters Kluwer Law & Business, periodical)
>
> Bonell, Michael Joachim and Anna Veneziano (eds), UNILEX: International Case Law & Bibliography on the UNIDROIT Principles of International Commercial Contracts[20] (Transnational Publishers Inc, loose-leaf)
>
> Coe, Jack Jr et al (eds), NAFTA Chapter Eleven Reports[21] (Kluwer Law International, periodical)
>
> Collection of ICC Awards/Recueil des sentences arbitrales de la ICC (Kluwer Law & Taxation, series)[22]
>
> Crawford, James et al (eds), ICSID Reports[23] (Cambridge University Press, periodical)
>
> Jarvin, Sigvard and Annette Magnusson (eds), *SCC Arbitral Awards 1999–2003* (Juris Publishing, 2006)
>
> Journal de Droit International[24] (JurisClasseur, periodical)
>
> Lee, Karen (ed), Iran-U.S. Claims Tribunal Reports (Cambridge University Press, periodical)
>
> Lloyd's Arbitration Reports[25] (Lloyd's of London Press, periodical)

---

20 UNILEX is primarily a free, fully searchable electronic database containing court cases and arbitral awards relating to the Convention on the International Sales of Goods ('CISG') and the UNIDROIT Principles of International Commercial Contracts. The electronic version can be accessed at <http://www.unilex.info/>.

21 The first volume in this series contains the primary materials for NAFTA dispute resolution, while subsequent volumes contain awards and court decisions.

22 This is a series of texts, containing awards from four-year blocks of time, compiled by various editors.

23 The International Centre for the Settlement of Investment Disputes ('ICSID') provides electronic access to decisions under the ICSID Convention at <http://icsid.worldbank.org/ICSID/FrontServlet?requestType=CasesRH&actionVal=ShowHome&pageName=Cases_Home>.

24 This journal—also known as 'Clunet' after its founder, Edouard Clunet—includes both commentary (which is typically in French) and extracts of ICC arbitral awards (usually in both French and English).

25 This reporting series was only active from 1988 to 1992.

Reeb, Matthieu (ed), Recueil des sentences du TAS/Digest of CAS Awards[26] (Kluwer Law International, series)

Reports of International Arbitral Awards/Recueil des sentences arbitrales[27] (United Nations, Office of Legal Affairs, periodical)

Rose, FD and FMB Reynolds (eds), Lloyd's Maritime and Commercial Law Quarterly (Lloyd's of London Press, periodical)

Scott, James Brown (ed), *The Hague Court Reports: Comprising the Awards, Accompanied by Syllabi, the Agreements for Arbitration, and Other Documents Presented in Each Case Submitted to the Permanent Court of Arbitration* (William S Hein & Co, 2004)

Smit, Hans and Vratislav Pechota (eds), World Arbitration Reporter, Vols II, IIA, IIB, III, IIIA, IIIB, IV, and IVA (Juris Publishing, loose-leaf)

Thomas, Christopher and Cameron Mowatt (eds), NAFTA Arbitration Reports[28] (Cameron May Ltd, loose-leaf)

van den Berg, Albert Jan (ed), Yearbook Commercial Arbitration (Kluwer Law International, annual)[29]

H. Case Law

Case law consists of judicial opinions issued from national courts. Unlike arbitral awards, which have no precedential value, case law can be binding on judges who sit in the same jurisdiction whence the original decision was issued. Case law may also be binding on arbitrators, if the issue is one that is governed by national substantive or procedural law. However, case law will often be persuasive to both judges and arbitrators in other circumstances as well, so it behooves researchers to consider judicial opinions from a variety of jurisdictions whenever there is a disputed question of substantive law or procedure. **5.23**

---

[26] The CAS is the Court of Arbitration for Sport. There are three volumes of this publication, with the first covering awards from 1986 to 1998, the second covering awards from 1998 to 2000, and the third covering awards from 2001 to 2003.

[27] Access to the electronic version of this document is available at <http://www.un.org/law/riaa/>.

[28] Electronic access to NAFTA awards and decisions can be found at <http://www.sice.oas.org/DISPUTE/nafdispe.asp>.

[29] The tables of contents for all of the Yearbooks (which were first published in 1976 and are put out by the International Council for Commercial Arbitration ('ICCA')) can be found at <http://www.arbitration-icca.org/publications/yearbook_table_of_contents.html>. Furthermore, a consolidated list of arbitral awards included in the Yearbooks can be found at <http://www.arbitration-icca.org/media/0/12126757832960/final_list_of_awards.pdf>. The consolidated list of arbitral awards relating to investment treaties and published in the Yearbook Commercial Arbitration can be found at <http://www.arbitration-icca.org/media/0/12127369880360/iia_digest_investment_awards.pdf>.

5.24　Case law is reproduced in series of reports that are gathered and digested by official state sources or commercial publishers. Every state has one or more 'official' case reporting series, but lawyers may also use cases from 'unofficial' reporting series that either circulate judicial decisions more rapidly than the official reporting series[30] or that include opinions that are not included among the 'official' reports.[31] These 'unofficial' decisions may not carry the same weight as an 'official' decision or may not reflect the final language of the opinion, so advocates should be cautious about relying on unofficial and particularly unreported decisions unless they fully understand their use and value within the national judicial system.

5.25　Researchers can also locate judicial opinions in the electronic databases (both general and arbitration-specific) listed above under 'Specialized Electronic Databases' and the free websites listed in paragraph 5.16 under 'National Laws'. Furthermore, UNCITRAL supports an electronic database carrying case law on UNCITRAL texts, also known as CLOUT.[32]

5.26　Practitioners in international commercial arbitration often do not need or want access to the entire body of nation's court decisions, however. Instead, advocates only wish to review judicial opinions relevant to international arbitration, either in their home or foreign jurisdictions. Fortunately, there are a number of reporting series and compilation texts that cater to these particular needs, including the following:[33]

>　Alford, Roger (ed), World Trade and Arbitration Materials (Kluwer Law International, periodical)

---

[30] For example, in the United States, the 'official' reporting series for the United States Supreme Court—United States Reports (abbreviated 'US')—is quite slow. Practitioners routinely cite to privately published reports—including Supreme Court Reporter (abbreviated 'SCt'), United States Supreme Court Reports, Lawyers' Edition (abbreviated 'LEd') or United States Law Week (abbreviated 'USLW')—while waiting for the official reports to come out. Practitioners also must distinguish between official and unofficial reporting series for lower federal court decisions as well as state court decisions. As a rule, there are no differences in content between the official and unofficial versions of US judicial opinions. The situation is somewhat different in England and Wales, where there can be slight variations in language between different reports. Although the variations are not intended to be significant, practitioners may wish to be particularly careful about using the official text when closely parsing quoted excerpts to support their position on a closely contested question of English law.

[31] The advent of electronic legal databases has drastically increased researchers' access to unpublished decisions. In particular, the two major electronic publishers—Westlaw and LexisNexis—have made it a practice of including unpublished opinions in search results. This can be helpful to researchers in international arbitration to the extent that it increases the universe of potentially relevant authority, but it also makes the research process more expensive, time consuming, and potentially contentious, as advocates have more ammunition for argument.

[32] This database can be accessed free of charge on <http://www.uncitral.org/uncitral/en/case_law.html>.

[33] Space limitations require the restriction of this list to specialist arbitral reporters, but a more comprehensive list of the official reporting series of a wide variety of states can be found in Tables 1 and 2 of *The Bluebook: A Uniform System of Citation* (Harvard Law Review Association, 2006).

Alvarez, Henri C and David W Rivkin (eds), *Model Law Decisions: Cases Applying the UNCITRAL Model Law on International Commercial Arbitration* (Kluwer Law International, 2002)

ASA Bulletin (Wolters Kluwer Law & Business, periodical)

Bonell, Michael Joachim and Anna Veneziano (eds), UNILEX: International Case Law & Bibliography on the UNIDROIT Principles of International Commercial Contracts[34] (Transnational Publishers Inc, loose-leaf)

Brand, Ronald A et al (eds), *The Draft UNCITRAL Digest and Beyond* (Sweet & Maxwell, 2003)

Coe, Jack Jr et al (eds), NAFTA Chapter Eleven Reports[35] (Kluwer Law International, periodical)

Jarvin, Sigvard and Annette Magnusson (eds), *International Arbitration Court Decisions* (Juris Net LLC, 2008)

Mealey's Litigation Reports: Reinsurance (LexisNexis, electronic or loose-leaf)

Mealey's International Arbitration Report (LexisNexis, electronic or loose-leaf)

Model Law Materials (formerly Model Arbitration Law Quarterly Reports) (interarb, periodical)

Patocchi, Paolo Michele and Matthias Scherer (eds), *The Swiss International Arbitration Law Reports* (Juris Publishing, 2009)

Rose, FD and FMB Reynolds (eds), Lloyd's Maritime and Commercial Law Quarterly (Lloyd's of London Press, periodical)

Smit, Hans and Vratislav Pechota (eds), *International Commercial Arbitration and the Courts* (Juris Net LLC, 2006)

Smit, Hans and Vratislav Pechota (eds), World Arbitration Reporter, Vol V (Juris Publishing, loose-leaf)

van den Berg, Albert Jan (ed), Yearbook Commercial Arbitration (Kluwer Law International, annual)[36]

---

[34] UNILEX is primarily a free, fully searchable electronic database concerning court cases and arbitral awards relating to the Convention on the International Sales of Goods ('CISG') and the UNIDROIT Principles of International Commercial Contracts. The electronic version can be accessed at <http://www.unilex.info/>.

[35] The first volume in this series contains the primary materials for NAFTA dispute resolution, while subsequent volumes contain awards and court decisions.

[36] The tables of contents for all of the Yearbooks (which were first published in 1976 and are put out by the International Council for Commercial Arbitration ('ICCA')) can be found at <http://www.arbitration-icca.org/publications/yearbook_table_of_contents.html>. Furthermore, a consolidated list of court decisions included in the Yearbooks can be found at <http://www.arbitration-icca.org/publications/consolidated_list_of_all_court_decisions.html>. A consolidated list of cases

I. Treatises and Monographs

5.27 Treatises and monographs provide excellent and often detailed discussions of arbitration law and procedure. In addition to their independent analyses, many treatises also include reprints of relevant and often-used international conventions, statutes, and arbitral rules in their appendices. Student casebooks and hornbooks have been excluded from the following list of materials, even though many are written by eminent scholars, on the grounds that any discussion in those texts is aimed at a more basic level than is appropriate for practitioners and arbitrators.

> Abdalla El Sheikh, Fath El Rahman, *The Legal Regime of Foreign Private Investment in Sudan and Saudi Arabia* (Cambridge University Press, 2003)
>
> Aldridge, George H, *The Jurisprudence of the Iran-United States Claims Tribunal* (Clarendon Press, 1996)
>
> Al Tamini, Essam, *Practical Guide to Litigation and Arbitration in the United Arab Emirates* (Kluwer Law International, 2003)
>
> Ambrose, Clare and Karen Maxwell, *London Maritime Arbitration* (Informa UK Ltd, 2002)
>
> American Arbitration Association, ADR and the Law (Juris Publishing, annual)[37]
>
> American Arbitration Association, *Arbitration and the Law: American Arbitration Association 1993–94* (Juris Publishing, 1999)[38]
>
> American Law Institute/UNIDROIT, *Principles of Transnational Civil Procedure* (Cambridge University Press, 2007)
>
> Anton, AE and Paul R Beaumont, *Private International Law* (W Green, 1990)
>
> Arbitration and Mediation Institute of Canada, *The Arbitration Practice Handbook* (Arbitration and Mediation Institute of Canada, 1996)
>
> Arnold, Tom et al, *Patent Alternative Dispute Resolution Handbook* (Clark Boardman Callaghan, 1991)
>
> Asouzu, Amazu A, *International Commercial Arbitration and African States: Practice, Participation, and Institutional Development* (Cambridge University Press, 2001)

---

commenting on the New York Convention can be found at <http://www.arbitration-icca.org/publications/ny_convention_commentary_cases.html>.

[37] This is an annual publication, and the twenty-second volume was issued in 2008. Each year, the book reviews the previous year's significant developments in international arbitration.

[38] There are three volumes in this series, with the two previous editions covering the years 1991–1992 and 1992–1993.

Aspatore Books Staff, *International Arbitration: A Country by Country Look at Alternative Dispute Resolution Methods Around the Globe* (Aspatore Books, 2005)

Astor, Hilary and Christine Chinkin, *Dispute Resolution in Australia* (Butterworths, 2002)

Avanessian, Aida B, *Iran-United States Claims Tribunal in Action* (Brill Academic Publishers, 1993)

Bader, W Reece, Securities Arbitration: Practice and Forms (Juris Publishing, loose-leaf)

Baker, Ellis and Anthony Lavers, *Case in Point—Expert Witness* (RICS Books, 2005)

Baker, Stewart Abercrombie and Mark David Davis, *The UNCITRAL Arbitration Rules in Practice: The Experience of the Iran-United States Claims Tribunal* (Kluwer Law International, 1992)

Barin, Babak et al, *The Osler Guide to Commercial Arbitration in Canada: A Practical Introduction to Domestic and International Commercial Arbitration* (Kluwer Law International, 2006)

Barnett, Peter R, *Res Judicata, Estoppel, and Foreign Judgments: The Preclusive Effect of Foreign Judgments in Private International Law* (Oxford University Press, 2001)

Beaumont, Ben, *Arbitration and Rent Review* (EG Books, 2004)

Beaumont, Ben and Philip Yang, *Chinese Maritime Law and Arbitration* (Simmonds & Hill Publications, 1994)

Bell, Andrew S, *Forum Shopping and Venue Shopping in Transnational Litigation* (Oxford University Press, 2003)

Berger, Klaus Peter, *Arbitration Interactive* (Peter Lang, 2002)

Berger, Klaus Peter, *The Creeping Codification of Lex Mercatoria* (Kluwer Law International, 1993)

Berger, Klaus Peter, *International Economic Arbitration* (Kluwer Law & Taxation, 1993)

Berger, Klaus Peter, *Private Dispute Resolution in International Business: Negotiation, Mediation, Arbitration* (Kluwer Law International, 2006)

Berger, Klaus Peter and Catherine Kessedjian, *Forum Internationale: The New German Arbitration Law in International Perspective* (Kluwer Law International, 2000)

Bergsten, Eric E, International Commercial Arbitration (Oxford University Press, loose-leaf)

Bergsten, Eric E, International Commercial Arbitration Pacific Rim (Oxford University Press, loose-leaf)

Bernardini, Piero, *The Italian Law on Arbitration: Text and Notes* (Kluwer Law International, 1998)

Biehler, Gernot, *International Law in Practice: An Irish Perspective* (Round Hall, 2005)

Binder, Peter, *International Commercial Arbitration and Conciliation in UNCITRAL Model Law Jurisdictions* (Sweet & Maxwell, 2005)

Binder, Peter, *International Commercial Arbitration in UNCITRAL Model Law Jurisdictions: An International Comparison of the UNCITRAL Model Law on International Commercial Arbitration* (Sweet & Maxwell, 2000)

Bishop, R Doak et al, *Foreign Investment Disputes* (Kluwer Law International, 2005)

Blanke, Gordon, *The Use and Utility of International Arbitration in EC Commission Merger Remedies* (Europa Law Publishing, 2006)

Blessing, Marc, *Arbitrating Antitrust and Merger Control Issues* (Helbing & Lichtenhahn, 2003)

Blessing, Marc, *Introduction to Arbitration—Swiss and International Perspectives* (Helbing & Lichtenhahn, 1999)

Böckstiegel, Karl-Heinz et al, *Arbitration in Germany: The Model Law in Practice* (Kluwer Law International, 2008)

Borchers, Patrick J and Joachim Zekoll, *International Conflict of Laws for the Third Millennium* (Transnational Publishers, 2001)

Born, Gary B, *International Arbitration and Forum Selection Agreements: Drafting and Enforcing* (Kluwer Law International, 2006)

Born, Gary B, *International Commercial Arbitration* (Kluwer Law International, 2008)

Born, Gary B and Peter B Rutledge, *International Civil Litigation in United States Courts* (Aspen Publishers, 2007)

Bowman, John P, *Panama Convention & Its Implementation Under the Federal Arbitration Act* (Kluwer Law International, 2002)

Brand, Ronald A and Scott R Jablonski, *Forum Non Conveniens: History, Global Practice, and Future Under the Hague Convention on Choice of Court Agreements* (Oxford University Press, 2007)

Briggs, Adrian, *Agreements on Jurisdiction and Choice of Law* (Oxford University Press, 2008)

Brooke, Nicholas, *The French Code of Civil Procedure in English, 2007* (Oxford University Press, 2007)

Brower, Charles N and Jason D Brueschke, *The Iran-United States Claims Tribunal* (Kluwer Law International, 1998)

Brown, Chester, *A Common Law of International Adjudication* (Oxford University Press, 2007)

Brown, Henry and Arthur Marriott, *ADR: Principles and Practice* (Sweet & Maxwell, 1999)

Brown, Ronald C, *Understanding Chinese Courts and Legal Processes: Law With Chinese Characteristics* (Kluwer Law International, 1997)

Brunet, Edward et al, *Arbitration Law in America: A Critical Assessment* (Cambridge University Press, 2006)

Bucher, Andreas and Pierre-Yves Tschanz, *International Arbitration in Switzerland* (Helbing & Lichtenhahn, 1989)

Bühler, Michael, *The German Arbitration Act 1997: Text and Notes* (Kluwer Law International, 1998)

Bühler, Michael and Thomas H Webster, *Handbook of ICC Arbitration: Commentary, Precedents, Materials* (Sweet & Maxwell, 2008)

Bühring-Uhle, Christian et al, *Arbitration and Mediation in International Business: Designing Procedure for Effective Conflict Management* (Kluwer Law International, 2006)

Bui, Victoria et al, *International Dispute Resolution* (Sweet & Maxwell, 2004)

Caller, Russell, *ADR and Commercial Disputes* (Sweet & Maxwell, 2001)

Cameron, Peter, *International Energy Investment Law: The Pursuit of Stability* (Oxford University Press, 2009)

Campbell, Dennis and Bryan Birkeland, *Lawyering in the International Market* (Transnational Publishers, 1999)

Carbonneau, Thomas E, *Employment Arbitration* (Juris Publishing, 2006)

Carbonneau, Thomas E, *The Law and Practice of Arbitration* (Juris Publishing, 2007)

Caron, David D et al, *The UNCITRAL Arbitration Rules: A Commentary* (Oxford University Press, 2006)

Casey, J Brian, International and Domestic Commercial Arbitration (Carswell Legal Publications, loose-leaf)

Casey, J Brian and Janet Mills, *Arbitration Law of Canada: Practice and Procedure* (Juris Publishing, 2005)

Cato, D Mark, *Arbitration Practice and Procedure: Interlocutory and Hearing Problems* (Informa Finance, 2002)

Cato, D Mark, *The Expert in Litigation and Arbitration* (LLP Professional, 1999)

Cato, D Mark, *The Sanctuary House Case* (LLP Professional, 1996)

Cato, D Mark, *So You Really Want to be an Arbitrator?* (LLP Professional, 1999)

Centre for International Legal Studies, International Execution Against Judgment Debtors (Oxford University Press, loose-leaf)

Chamlongrasdr, Dhisadee, *Foreign State Immunity and Arbitration* (Cameron May Ltd, 2007)

Chukwumerije, Okezie, *Choice of Law in International Commercial Arbitration* (Quorum Books, 1994)

Coe, Jack J, Jr, *International Commercial Arbitration: American Principles and Practice in a Global Context* (Transnational Publishers, 1997)

Collier, JG, *Conflict of Laws* (Cambridge University Press, 2001)

Collier, John and Vaughan Lowe, *The Settlement of Disputes in International Law: Institutions and Procedures* (Oxford University Press, 2000)

Collins, Lawrence et al, *Dicey, Collins & Morris on the Conflict of Laws* (Sweet & Maxwell, 2008)

Connerty, Anthony, *Manual of Dispute Resolution* (Commonwealth Secretariat, 2006)

Cooley, John W, *The Arbitrator's Handbook* (National Institute for Trial Advocacy, 2005)

Cordero Moss, Guidetta, *International Commercial Arbitration: Party Autonomy and Mandatory Rules* (Tano Aschehoug, 1999)

Coulson, Peter, *Construction Adjudication* (Oxford University Press, 2007)

Craig, W Lawrence et al, *Annotated Guide to the 1998 ICC Arbitration Rules With Commentary* (Oxford University Press, 1999)

Craig, W Lawrence et al, *International Chamber of Commerce Arbitration* (Oxford University Press, 2001)

Crawford, Elizabeth and Janeen Carruthers, *International Private Law in Scotland* (W Green, 2006)

Crowter, Henry and Simon Hughes, *Introduction to Arbitration* (Informa Publishing, 2006)

D'Ambrumenil, Peter L, *What is Dispute Resolution?* (LLP Professional, 1998)

Dauer, Edward A, ADR Law and Practice (Juris Publishing, loose-leaf)

Davidson, Fraser P, *Arbitration* (W Green, 2000)

Dejun, Cheng et al, *International Arbitration in the People's Republic of China: Commentary, Cases and Materials* (Butterworths Asia, 1995)

Delaume, George R, *Law and Practice of Transnational Contracts* (Oceana Publications, 1988)

de Pavia Muniz, Joaquim T and Ana Teresa Palhares Basilio, *Arbitration Law of Brazil: Practice and Procedure* (Juris Publishing, 2006)

Derains, Yves and Bryant Garth, *Dealing in Virtue—International Commercial Arbitration and the Construction of a Transnational Legal Order* (University of Chicago Press, 1996)

Derains, Yves and Eric A Schwartz, *A Guide to the ICC Rules of Arbitration* (Kluwer Law International, 2005)

de Roo, Anne and Rob Jagtenberg, *Settling Labour Disputes in Europe* (Kluwer Law International, 1994)

Dev, Kohli Hari, *New Case Law Referencer on Arbitration and Conciliation Act* (Universal Law Publishing Co Pvt Ltd, 2008)

Devolvé, Jean-Luis et al, *French Arbitration Law & Practice* (Kluwer Law International, 2003)

Dezalay, Yves and Brian G Garth, *Dealing in Virtue: International Commercial Arbitration and the Construction of a Transnational Legal Order* (University of Chicago Press, 1998)

di Petro, Domenico and Martin Platte, *Enforcement of International Arbitration Awards: The New York Convention of 1958* (Cameron May Ltd, 2001)

Dispute Resolution Faculty, *Surveyors Acting as Arbitrators and as Independent Experts in Commercial Property Rent Reviews* (RICS Books, 2007)

Dolzer, Rudolph and Christoph Schreur, *Principles of International Investment Law* (Oxford University Press, 2008)

Dore, Isaak I, *Arbitration and Conciliation under the UNCITRAL Rules: A Textual Analysis* (Kluwer Academic Publishers, 1986)

Dore, Isaak I, *Theory and Practice of Multiparty Commercial Arbitration, With Special Reference to the UNCITRAL Framework* (Springer, 1990)

Dore, Isaak I, *The UNCITRAL Framework for Arbitration in Contemporary Perspective* (Graham & Trotman, 1993)

Dugan, Christopher et al, *Investor-State Arbitration* (Oxford University Press, 2009)

El-Ahdab, Abdul Hamid, *Arbitration With the Arab Countries* (Kluwer Law International, 1998)

Fawcett, James et al, *Private International Law* (Oxford University Press, 2008)

Fellas, John, *Transatlantic Commercial Litigation and Arbitration* (Oxford University Press, 2004)

Fentiman, Richard, *International Commercial Litigation* (Oxford University Press, 2008)

Fiadjoe, Albert, *Alternative Dispute Resolution* (Routledge Cavendish, 2004)

Fletcher, C Edward, *Arbitrating Securities Disputes* (Practising Law Institute, 1990)

Folberg, Jay et al, *Resolving Disputes Theory, Practice, and Law* (Aspen Publishers, 2005)

Forde, Michael, *Arbitration Law & Procedure* (Round Hall Press, 1994)

Fox, Hazel, *The Law of State Immunity* (Oxford University Press, 2008)

Fox, William F, Jr, *International Commercial Agreements: A Functional Primer on Drafting, Negotiating and Resolving Disputes* (Kluwer Law International, 1998)

Franklin, David, *International Commercial Debt Collection* (Carswell, 2007)

Frick, Joachim G, *Arbitration in Complex International Contracts* (Kluwer Law International, 2001)

Friedland, Paul D, *Arbitration Clauses for International Contracts* (Juris Publishing, 2007)

Fung, David R and Wang Shang Chung, *Arbitration in China: A Practical Guide* (Sweet & Maxwell Asia (Hong Kong), 2004)

Gabriel, Henry et al, *A Practical Guide to International Arbitration* (Oxford University Press, 2001)

Gaitskell, Robert, *Engineers' Dispute Resolution Handbook* (Thomas Telford Publishing, 2006)

Garro, Alejandro M, *Arbitration Law & Practice in Latin America* (Juris Publishing, 2001)

Gazzini, Isabelle Fellrath, *Cultural Property Disputes: The Role of Arbitration in Solving Non-Contractual Disputes* (Transnational Publishers, 2004)

Geeroms, Sofie, *Foreign Law in Civil Litigation: A Comparative and Functional Analysis* (Oxford University Press, 2004)

Gharavi, Hamid G, *The International Effectiveness of the Annulment of an Arbitral Award* (Kluwer Law International, 2002)

Gottschalk, Eckart et al, *Conflict of Laws in a Globalized World* (Cambridge University Press, 2007)

Grenig, Jay E, *Alternative Dispute Resolution* (Thomson/West, 2005)

Grigera Naón, Horacio A, *Choice of Law Problems in International Commercial Arbitration* (JCB Mohr, 1992)

Grubbs, Shelby R, *International Civil Procedure* (Kluwer Law International, 2003)

Guest, Jim, *Alternative Dispute Resolution Practice and Procedure* (Brookers, CD-ROM/online)

Håkansson, Cecilia, *Commercial Arbitration Under Chinese Law: International Commerce and Trade* (Coronet Books, 2000)

Hanotiau, Bernard, *Complex Arbitrations: Multi-Party, Multi-Contract, Multi-Issue, and Class Actions* (Kluwer Law International, 2006)

Harris, Bruce et al, *The Arbitration Act 1996: A Commentary* (Wiley-Blackwell, 2007)

Heilbron, Hilary, *A Practical Guide to International Arbitration in London* (Informa Publishing, 2008)

Hertz, Ketilbjorn, *Danish Arbitration Act 2005* (Djoef Publishing, 2005)

Heuman, Lars, *Arbitration Law of Sweden: Practice and Procedure* (Juris Publishing, 2003)

Heuman, Lars, *Current Issues in Swedish Arbitration* (Kluwer Academic Publishers Group, 1990)

Hibbard, Peter and Paul Newman, *Alternative Dispute Resolution (ADR) and Adjudication in Construction Disputes* (Wiley-Blackwell, 1999)

Hill, Jonathan, *International Commercial Disputes in English Courts* (Hart Publishing, 2005)

Hill, Jonathan, *The Law Relating to International Commercial Disputes* (LLP Ltd, 1998)

Hill, Marvin F and Anthony V Sinicropi, *Evidence in Arbitration* (BNA Books, 1987)

Hirsch, Moshe, *The Arbitration Mechanism of the International Centre for the Settlement of Investment Disputes* (Martinus Nijhoff Publishers, 1993)

Hobér, Kaj, *Enforcing Foreign Arbitral Awards Against Russian Entities* (Juris Publishing, 1999)

Hobér, Kaj, *Essays on International Arbitration* (Juris Publishing, 2006)

Hobér, Kaj, *Extinctive Prescription and Applicable Law in Interstate Arbitration* (Lustu Forlag, 2001)

Hobér, Kaj, *Investment Arbitration in Eastern Europe: In Search of a Definition of Expropriation* (Juris Publishing, 2007)

Hoblin, Philip J, *Securities Arbitration: Procedures, Strategies, Cases* (New York Institute of Finance, 1992)

Holbein, James R and Nick Ranieri, North-American Free Trade Agreements: Chapter 11 Investor-State Arbitration (Oxford University Press, loose-leaf)

Holtham, Diana et al, *Resolving Construction Disputes* (Chandos Publishing, 1999)

Holtzmann, Howard M and Joseph E Neuhaus, *A Guide to the UNCITRAL Model Law on International Commercial Arbitration: Legislative History and Commentary* (Kluwer Law & Taxation, 1989)

Hopkins, Roger and Benjamin John, *Arbitration Law Handbook* (LLP Professional, 2007)

Horne, Julia, *Cross-border Internet Dispute Resolution* (Cambridge University Press, 2009)

Huleatt-James, Mark and Nicholas Gould, *International Commercial Arbitration: A Handbook* (LLP Ltd, 1999)

Huleatt-James, Mark et al, *International Arbitration* (Informa Professional, 2004)

Hunter, Robert LC, *The Law of Arbitration in Scotland* (Tottel Publishing, 2002)

Hunter, Martin H and Toby Landau, *The English Arbitration Act 1996: Text and Notes* (Kluwer Law International, 1998)

I Alam Eldin, Mohie Eldin, *Arbitral Awards of the Cairo Regional Centre for International Commercial Arbitration* (Kluwer Law International, 1999)

I Alam Eldin, Mohie Eldin, *Arbitral Awards of the Cairo Regional Centre for International Commercial Arbitration, Volume II* (Brill Academic Publishers, 2003)

Institution of Chemical Engineers, *Forms of Contract Arbitration Rules—The Pink Book* (Institution of Chemical Engineers, 2005)

Institution of Chemical Engineers, *ICE Arbitration Procedure 2006* (Thomas Telford Publishing, 2006)

International Bureau of the Permanent Court of Arbitration, *Arbitration in Air, Space and Telecommunication Law* (Kluwer Law International, 2002)

International Bureau of the Permanent Court of Arbitration, *Multiple Party Actions in International Arbitration: Consent, Procedure and Enforcement* (Oxford University Press, 2009)

International Bureau of the Permanent Court of Arbitration, *Redressing Injustices Through Mass Claims Processes: Innovative Responses to Unique Challenges* (Oxford University Press, 2006)

International Chamber of Commerce, *60 Years of ICC Arbitration* (ICC Publishing, 1984)

International Chamber of Commerce, *The Arbitral Process and the Independence of Arbitrators* (ICC Publishing, 2008)

International Chamber of Commerce, *Arbitration, Finance and Insurance* (ICC Publishing, 2001)

International Chamber of Commerce, *Competition and Arbitration Law* (ICC Publishing, 1993)

International Chamber of Commerce, *Conservatory and Provisional Measures in International Arbitration* (ICC Publishing, 1993)

International Chamber of Commerce, *Document Production in International Arbitration* (ICC Publishing, 2006)

International Chamber of Commerce, *Multi-Party Arbitration* (ICC Publishing, 1991)

International Chamber of Commerce, *Parallel State and Arbitral Procedures in International Arbitration* (ICC Publishing, 2005)

International Chamber of Commerce, *Taking of Evidence in International Proceedings* (ICC Publishing, 1990)

International Chamber of Commerce, *UNIDROIT Principles of International Commercial Contracts: A New Lex Mercatoria?* (ICC Publishing, 1995)

International Chamber of Commerce, *UNIDROIT Principles of International Commercial Contracts: New Developments and Applications* (ICC Publishing, 2005)

International Chamber of Commerce, *UNIDROIT Principles of International Commercial Contracts: Reflections on Their Use in International Arbitration* (ICC Publishing, 2002)

International Trade Centre, *Arbitration and Alternative Dispute Resolution: How to Settle International Business Disputes* (Radha Press, 2005)

Jacobs, Marcus, Jacobs Commercial Arbitration Law & Practice (Lawbook Co, loose-leaf)

Jacobs, Marcus, Jacobs International Commercial Arbitration in Australia (Lawbook Co, loose-leaf)

Jacobs, Richard et al, *Liability Insurance in International Arbitration: The Bermuda Form* (Hart Publishing, 2004)

Jaksic, Aleksander, *Arbitration and Human Rights* (Peter Lang Publishing Group, 2002)

Jasper, Margaret, *The Law of Dispute Resolution: Arbitration and Alternative Dispute Resolution* (Oxford University Press, 2000)

Jenkins, Jane and Simon Stebbings, *International Construction Arbitration Law* (Kluwer Law International, 2006)

Johnson, Derek K, *International Commodity Arbitration* (LLP Ltd, 1991)

Joseph, David, *Jurisdiction and Arbitration Agreements and Their Enforcement* (Sweet & Maxwell, 2005)

Juenger, Frederich K, *Selected Essays on the Conflict of Laws* (Transnational Publishers, 2000)

Kantor, Mark, *Valuation for Arbitration* (Kluwer Law International, 2008)

Karsten, Kristine and Andrew Berkeley, *Arbitration: Corruption, Money Laundering and Fraud* (Kluwer Law International, 2006)

Katsch, Ethan and Janet Rifkin, *Online Dispute Resolution: Conflict Resolution in Cyberspace* (Jossey Bass, 2001)

Kaufmann-Kohler, Gabrielle, *Arbitration at the Olympics: Issues of Fast-Track Dispute Resolution and Sports Law* (Kluwer Law International, 2001)

Kaufmann-Kohler, Gabrielle, *Online Dispute Resolution: Challenges for Contemporary Justice* (Kluwer Law International, 2004)

Kendall, John et al, *Expert Determination* (Sweet & Maxwell, 2008)

Kimmelman, Louis and Dana MacGrath, *Judicial Review of Commercial Arbitration Awards in the United States* (Oxford University Press, 2009)

Kinnear, Meg et al, *Investment Disputes Under NAFTA: An Annotated Guide to NAFTA Chapter 11* (Kluwer Law International, 2006)

Klein, Natalie, *Dispute Settlement in the UN Convention on the Law of the Sea* (Cambridge University Press, 2005)

Kleinheisterkamp, Jan, *International Commercial Arbitration in Latin America: Regulation and Practice in MERCOSUR and the Associated Countries* (Oxford University Press, 2005)

Konigsberg, Alexander S, *International Franchising* (Juris Publishing, 2008)

Koster, John C et al, *Benedict on Admiralty* (Matthew Bender, loose-leaf)

Kreindler, Richard, *Transnational Litigation: A Basic Primer* (Oxford University Press, 1999)

Kruger, Thalia, *Civil Jurisdiction Rules of the EU and Their Impact on Third States* (Oxford University Press, 2008)

Kumar, Bansal Ashwinie, *Arbitration Agreements and Awards* (Universal Law Publishing Co Pvt Ltd, 2006)

Kurkela, Matti, *Due Process in International Commercial Arbitration* (Oxford University Press, 2006)

Kwatra, GK, *Arbitration and Alternative Dispute Resolution* (Universal Law Publishing Co Pvt Ltd, 2008)

Kwatra, GK, *Arbitration and Conciliation Law of India* (Universal Law Publishing Co Pvt Ltd, 2008)

Kwatra, GK, *Arbitration and Contract Law in SAARC Countries* (Universal Law Publishing Co Pvt Ltd, 2008)

Kwatra, GK, *Arbitration Made Easy: A Practical Guide* (Universal Law Publishing Co Pvt Ltd, 2008)

Kwatra, GK, *Case Law on UNCITRAL Model Law on International Commercial Arbitration (With Reference to Corresponding Provisions of the New Indian Arbitration Law)* (Universal Law Publishing Co Pvt Ltd, 2004)

Landolt, Philip, *Modernised EC Competition Law in International Arbitration* (Kluwer Law International, 2006)

Lazič, Vesna, *Insolvency Proceedings and Commercial Arbitration* (Kluwer Law International, 1998)

LEADER Association of Dispute Resolvers, Australasian Dispute Resolution Service (Lawbook Co, loose-leaf)

Leathley, Christian, *International Dispute Resolution in Latin America: An Institutional Overview* (Kluwer Law International, 2007)

Legislative Affairs Commission of the People's Republic of China, *Arbitration Law of China* (Sweet & Maxwell Asia, 1997)

Lew, Julian DM et al, *Comparative International Commercial Arbitration* (Kluwer Law International, 2003)

Liebscher, Christoph, *The Austrian Arbitration Act 2006: Text and Notes* (Kluwer Law International, 2006)

Liebscher, Christoph, *The Healthy Award: Challenge in International Commercial Arbitration* (Kluwer Law International, 2003)

Loh Sze On, Quentin and Edwin Lee Peng Khoon, *Confidentiality in Arbitration: How Far Does It Extend?* (Academy Publishing, 2007)

Lookofsky, Joseph M, *Transnational Litigation and Commercial Arbitration: A Comparative Analysis of American, European, and International Law* (Juris Publishing, 2004)

Lowenfeld, Andreas F, *International Litigation and Arbitration* (West Group, 2002)

Lowenfeld, Andreas F, *Lowenfeld on International Arbitration: Collected Essays Over Three Decades* (Juris Publishing, 2005)

Lynch, Katherine, *The Forces of Economic Globalization: Challenges to the Regime of International Commercial Arbitration* (Kluwer Law International, 2003)

Ma, The Honourable Mr Justice, *Arbitration in Hong Kong: A Practical Guide* (Sweet & Maxwell Asia (Hong Kong), 2003)

MacDonald, Charles and Chirag Karia, *Butterworths Commercial Court & Arbitration Pleadings* (Tottel Publishing Ltd, 2005)

Mackie, Karl et al, *The ADR Practice Guide: Commercial Dispute Resolution* (Tottel Publishing Ltd, 2007)

Macneil, Ian R, *American Arbitration Law: Reformation, Nationalization, Internationalization* (Oxford University Press, 1992)

Macneil, Ian R et al, *Federal Arbitration Law: Agreements, Awards, and Remedies Under the Federal Arbitration Act* (Little, Brown, 1994)

Madsen, Finn, *Commercial Arbitration in Sweden* (Oxford University Press, 2007)

Mann, FA, *Notes and Comments on Cases in International Law, Commercial Law, and Arbitration* (Oxford University Press, 1993)

Mapp, Wayne, *The Iran-United States Tribunal: The First Ten Years, 1981–1991: An Assessment of the Tribunal's Jurisprudence and Its Contribution to International Arbitration* (Manchester University Press, 1993)

Marboe, Irmgard, *Calculation of Compensation and Damages in International Investment Law* (Oxford University Press, 2009)

Marshall, Enid A, *Gill: The Law of Arbitration* (Sweet & Maxwell, 2001)

McConnaughay, Philip J and Thomas A Ginsburg, *International Commercial Arbitration in Asia* (Juris Net LLC, 2006)

McLachlan, Campbell et al, *International Investment Principles: Substantive Principles* (Oxford University Press, 2008)

Merkin, Robert M, *Arbitration Act—An Annotated Guide* (LLP Ltd, 2000)

Merkin, Robert M, *Arbitration Law* (LLP Ltd, 2004)

Merrills, JG, *International Dispute Settlement* (Cambridge University Press, 2005)

Mohebi, Mohsen, *The International Law Character of the Iran-United States Claims Tribunal* (Kluwer Law International, 1999)

Morrissey, Joseph F and Jack M Graves, *International Sales Law and Arbitration: Problems, Cases and Commentary* (Kluwer Law International, 2008)

Moser, Michael, *Managing Business Disputes in Today's China: Duelling with Dragons* (Kluwer Law International, 2007)

Moser, Michael and Teresa YW Cheng, *Arbitration in Hong Kong: A User's Guide* (Kluwer Law International, 2004)

Moses, Margaret L, *The Principles and Practice of International Commercial Arbitration* (Cambridge University Press, 2008)

Mouri, Allahyar, *The International Law of Expropriation as Reflected in the Work of the Iran-U.S. Claims Tribunal* (Martinus Nijhoff Publishers, 1993)

Müller, Christoph, *International Arbitration: A Guide to the Complete Swiss Case Law (Unreported and Reported)* (Schulthess Juristische Medien, 2004)

Mustill, Michael J et al, *Mustill & Boyd: Commercial Arbitration* (Butterworths Law, 2008)

Mustill, Michael J and Stewart C Boyd, *The Law and Practice of Commercial Arbitration in England* (Lexis Law Publications, 1989)

Nathan, KVSK, *The ICSID Convention: The Law of the International Centre for Settlement of Investment Disputes* (Juris Publishing, 2000)

Newman, Lawrence W and Michael Burrows, The Practice of International Litigation (Juris Publishing, loose-leaf)

Noortmann, Math, *Enforcing International Law; From Self-Help to Self-Contained* (Ashgate Publishing Co, 2005)

Nygh, Peter, *Autonomy in International Contracts* (Clarendon Press, 1999)

Nygh, Peter, *Choice of Forum and Laws in International Commercial Arbitration* (Kluwer Law International, 1997)

O'Meara, Daniel P, *O'Meara Employment Arbitration* (Matthew Bender, 2007)

O'Reilly, Michael, *Costs in Arbitration Proceedings* (LLP Professional Publishing, 1997)

Oser, David, *The UNIDROIT Principles of International Commercial Contracts: A Governing Law?* (Martinus Nijhoff Publishers, 2008)

Ottolenghi, Smadar, *The Law of Arbitration in Israel* (Kluwer Law International, 2002)

Palmer, Michael and Simon Roberts, *Law in Context: Dispute Processes—ADR and the Primary Forms of Decision Making* (Cambridge University Press, 2005)

Pamplin, Chris, *Expert Witness Fees* (JS Publications, 2007)

Pamplin, Chris, *Expert Witness Practice in the Civil Arena* (JS Publications, 2007)

Park, William W, *Arbitration of International Business Disputes: Studies in Law and Practice* (Oxford University Press, 2006)

Park, William W, *International Forum Selection* (Kluwer Law International, 1995)

Patridge, Mark VB, *Alternative Dispute Resolution: How to Use ADR to Achieve Better Results and Lower Costs* (Oxford University Press, 2009)

Paulsson, Jan et al, *The Freshfields Guide to Arbitration and ADR: Clauses in International Contracts* (Aspen Publishers, 1999)

Pellonpää, Matti and David D Caron, *The UNCITRAL Arbitration Rules as Interpreted and Applied: Selected Problems in Light of the Practice of the Iran-United States Claims Tribunal* (Finnish Lawyers' Publishing, 1994)

Permanent Court of Arbitration, *The Bank for International Settlements Arbitration Awards of 2002 and 2003* (Cambridge University Press, 2007)

Permanent Court of Arbitration, *The Eritrea-Yemen Arbitration Awards 1998 and 1999* (Cambridge University Press, 2005)

Permanent Court of Arbitration, *The Iron-Rhine (IJzeren Rijn) Arbitration (Belgium-Netherlands) Award of 2005* (Cambridge University Press, 2007)

Permanent Court of Arbitration, *Labor Law Beyond Borders: ADR and the Internationalization of Labor Dispute Settlement* (Kluwer Law International, 2003)

Permanent Court of Arbitration, *The Resolution of Cultural Property Disputes* (Kluwer Law International, 2004)

Permanent Court of Arbitration, *The Rhine Chlorides Arbitration Concerning the Auditing of Accounts (Netherlands-France) Award of 2004* (Cambridge University Press, 2008)

Peter, Henry, *Arbitration in the America's Cup* (Kluwer Law International, 2004)

Peter, Wolfgang, *Arbitration & Renegotiation of International Investment Agreements* (Kluwer Law International, 1995)

Petrochilos, Georgios, *Procedural Law in International Arbitration* (Oxford University Press, 2004)

Petsche, Markus A, *The Growing Autonomy of International Commercial Arbitration* (Sellier European Law Publishers, 2005)

Plant, David W, *Resolving International Intellectual Property Disputes* (ICC Publishing, 1999)

Poudret, Jean-Francois and Sebastien Besson, *Comparative Law of International Arbitration* (Sweet & Maxwell, 2007)

Powell-Smith, Vincent et al, *Construction Arbitrations* (Blackwell Science Ltd, 2000)

Prujiner, Alain and Bernard Coles, *Treaties and International Documents Used in International Trade* (ICC Publishing, 1995)

Rahmatullah, Khan, *The Iran-United States Claims Tribunal: Controversies, Cases, and Contribution* (Martinus Nijhoff Publishers, 1990)

Rao, PC and William Sheffield, *Alternative Dispute Resolution: What it is and How it Works* (Universal Law Publishing Co Pvt Ltd, 2007)

Raphael, Thomas, *The Anti-Suit Injunctions* (Oxford University Press, 2008)

Redfern, Alan and Martin Hunter et al, *Law and Practice of International Commercial Arbitration* (Sweet & Maxwell, 2004)

Reed, Lucy et al, *A Guide to ICSID Arbitration* (Kluwer Law International, 2004)

Reigler, Stefan et al, *Arbitration Law of Austria: Practice and Procedure* (Juris Publishing, 2007)

Reimann, Mathias, *Conflict of Laws in Western Europe: A Guide Through the Jungle* (Transnational Publishers, 1995)

Reinisch, August, *Standards of Protection in International Investment Law* (Oxford University Press, 2008)

Reisman, W Michael, *Systems of Control in International Adjudication and Arbitration* (Duke University Press, 1992)

Reisman, W Michael et al, *International Commercial Arbitration* (Foundation Press, 1997)

Reynolds, Michael P, *The Expert Witness in Construction Disputes* (Blackwell Science, 2001)

Rhoades, Rufus V et al, *The Practitioner's Handbook on International Arbitration and Mediation* (Juris Publishing Inc, 2002)

Riches, John and Christopher Doncaster, *Construction Adjudication* (Blackwell Publishing, 2004)

Rivkin, David W and Charles Platto, *Litigation and Arbitration in Central and Eastern Europe* (Kluwer Law International, 1998)

Roberts, Simon and Michael Palmer, *Dispute Processes: ADR and the Primary Forms of Decision-Making* (Cambridge University Press, 2005)

Rodriguez, Suzanne and Bertrand Prell, *International Judicial Assistance in Civil Matters* (Transnational Publishers, 1999)

Roebuck, Derek, *The Charitable Arbitrator* (Holo Books, 2002)

Rogers, Catherine, *Ethics in International Arbitration* (Oxford University Press, 2009)

Rowley, J William, *Arbitration World—Jurisdictional Comparison* (The European Lawyer, 2004)

Rubino-Sammartano, Mauro, *International Arbitration Law and Practice* (Kluwer Law International, 2001)

Rubins, Noah and N Stephan Kinsella, *International Investment, Political Risk and Dispute Resolution: A Practitioner's Guide* (Oceana Publications, 2005)

Rule, Colin, *Online Dispute Resolution for Business* (Jossey Bass, 2002)

Rutherford, Margaret and John Sims, *Arbitration Act 1996: A Practical Guide* (FT Law & Tax, 1996)

Saleh, Samir, *Commercial Arbitration in the Arab Middle East: Shari'a, Lebanon, Syria, and Egypt* (Hart Publications, 2006)

Samuel, Adam, *Jurisdictional Problems in International Commercial Arbitration: A Study of Belgian, Dutch, English, French, Swedish, Swiss, US and West German Law* (Schulthess Polygraphischer Verlag, 1989)

Sanders, Pieter, *Quo Vadis Arbitration? Sixty Years of Arbitration Practice* (Kluwer Law International, 1999)

Sanders, Pieter, *The Work of UNCITRAL on Arbitration and Conciliation* (Kluwer Law International, 2004)

Sanders, Pieter and Albert Jan van den Berg, *The Netherlands Arbitration Act, 1986* (Springer, 1987)

Sato, Yasunobu, *Commercial Dispute Processing and Japan* (Kluwer Law International, 2001)

Savola, Mika, *Law and Practice of Arbitration in Finland* (Finnish Arbitration Association, 2004)

Sayeed, Abdulhay, *Corruption in International Trade and Commercial Arbitration* (Kluwer Law International, 2004)

Schäfer, Erik et al, *ICC Arbitration in Practice* (Kluwer Law International, 2004)

Schreuer, Christoph, *The ICSID Convention: A Commentary on the Convention on the Settlement of Investment Disputes Between States and Nationals of Other States* (Cambridge University Press, 2001)

Schultz, Thomas, *Arbitration and Information Technology: A Practitioner's Guide* (Kluwer Law International, 2006)

Schwebel, Stephen M, *International Arbitration: Three Salient Problems* (Cambridge University Press, 1993)

Shan, Wenhua and Norah Gallagher, *Chinese Investment Treaties: Policies and Practices* (Oxford University Press, 2008)

Shany, Yuval, *The Competing Jurisdictions of International Courts and Tribunals* (Oxford University Press, 2004)

Shelkoplyas, Natalaya, *The Application of EC Law in Arbitration Proceedings* (Europa Law Publishing, 2003)

Sheridan, Peter, *Construction and Engineering Arbitration* (Sweet & Maxwell, 1999)

Siig, Kristina Maria, *Arbitration Agreements* (DJOF Publishing, 2003)

Simpson, Thacher & Bartlett LLP, *Comparison of Asian International Arbitration Rules* (Juris Publishing, 2003)

Simpson, Thacher & Bartlett LLP, *Comparison of International Arbitration Rules* (Juris Publishing, 2002)

Smith, Richard Wilmont, *Construction Contracts Law and Practice* (Oxford University Press, 2006)

Snijders, Henk J, *Access to Civil Procedure Abroad* (Aspen Publishers, 1996)

Solovay, Norman and Cynthia K Reed, The Internet and Dispute Resolution: Untangling the Web (New Law Journal Press, loose-leaf)

Sornarajah, M, *International Commercial Arbitration: The Problem of State Contracts* (Longman Singapore, 1990)

Sornarajah, M, *The International Law on Foreign Investment* (Cambridge University Press, 2004)

Sornarajah, M, *The Settlement of Foreign Investment Disputes* (Kluwer Law International, 2000)

Sourdin, Tania, *Alternative Dispute Resolution* (Lawbook Co, 2008)

Spencer, David and Tom Altobelli, *Dispute Resolution in Australia: Cases, Commentary & Materials* (Lawbook Co, 2004)

Stephenson, Douglas S, *Arbitration Practice in Construction Contracts* (Wiley-Blackwell, 2001)

Stewart, David and Mark D Davis, *The UNCITRAL Rules in Practice: The Experience of the Iran-United States Claims Tribunal* (Kluwer Law International, 1992)

Storme, Marcel and Bernadette Demeulenaere, *International Commercial Arbitration in Belgium: A Handbook* (Springer, 1989)

Strong, SI, *Research and Practice in International Commercial Arbitration: Sources and Strategies* (Oxford University Press, 2009)

Subedi, Surya P, *International Investment Law: Reconciling Policy and Principle* (Hart Publishing, 2008)

Sutton, David St John et al, *Russell on Arbitration* (Sweet & Maxwell, 2007)

Tackaberry, John and Arthur Marriott, *Bernstein's Handbook on Arbitration and Dispute Resolution Practice* (Sweet & Maxwell, 2003)

Takahashi, Koji, *Claims for Contribution and Reimbursement in an International Context: Conflict of Law Dimensions of Third Party Procedure* (Oxford University Press, 2000)

Tao, Jingzhou, *Arbitration Law and Practice in China* (Kluwer Law International, 2004)

Thomas, D Rhidian, *Default Powers of Arbitrators: An Analysis of the Law and Practice Relating to the Default Powers of Arbitrators* (Informa Professional, 1996)

Thomas, D Rhidian, *The Law and Practice Relating to Appeals from Arbitration Awards* (Lloyd's of London Press Ltd, 1994)

Thompson, George and Lawrence Bogard, Transnational Contracts (Oxford University Press, loose-leaf)

Timmermans, Wim Albert, *Carriage of Goods by Sea in the Practice of the USSR Maritime Arbitration Commission* (Martinus Nijhoff Publishers, 1990)

Toope, Stephen J, *Mixed International Arbitration: Studies in Arbitration Between States and Private Persons* (Cambridge University Press, 1990)

Trakman, Leon E, *Dispute Settlement Under the NAFTA* (Transnational Pub Inc, 1997)

Turner, Peter and Reza Mohtashami, *A Guide to the LCIA Arbitration Rules* (Oxford University Press, 2009)

Turner, Ray, *Arbitration Awards: A Practical Approach* (Blackwell Publishing, 2005)

Tweeddale, Andrew and Karen Tweeddale, *A Practical Approach to Arbitration Law* (Blackstone Press, 1999)

Tweeddale, Andrew and Karen Tweeddale, *Arbitration of Commercial Disputes: International and English Law and Practice* (Oxford University Press, 2005)

United Nations Conference on Trade and Development, *Arbitration and Alternative Dispute Resolution: How to Settle International Business Disputes* (United Nations Publications, 2001)

United Nations Conference on Trade and Development, *Investor-State Disputes Arising from Investment Treaties: A Review* (United Nations Publications, 2007)

van den Berg, Albert Jan, *The New York Arbitration Convention of 1958: Toward a Uniform Judicial Interpretation* (Kluwer Law & Taxation, 1981)

van den Berg, Albert Jan et al, *Netherlands Arbitration Law* (Kluwer Law International, 1993)

van Harten, Gus, *Investment Treaty Arbitration and Public Law* (Oxford University Press, 2008)

van Hof, Jacomijn J, *Commentary on the UNCITRAL Arbitration Rules: The Applications by the Iran-United States Claims Tribunal* (Kluwer Law International, 1991)

van Rhee, CH, *European Traditions in Civil Procedure* (Hart Publishing, 2005)

Várady, Tibor, *Language and Translation in International Commercial Arbitration: From the Constitution of the Arbitral Tribunal Through Recognition and Enforcement Proceedings* (Cambridge University Press, 2006)

Vibhute, KI, *International Commercial Arbitration and State Immunity* (Butterworths, 1999)

Vicuña, Francisco Orrego, *International Dispute Settlement in an Evolving Global Society: Constitutionalization, Accessibility, and Privatization* (Cambridge University Press, 2004)

von Mehren, Arthur T and Eckart Gottschalk, *Adjudicatory Authority in Private International Law* (Martinus Nijhoff Publishers, 2007)

Wade, Shai and Stephen York, *A Commentary on the LCIA Rules* (Sweet & Maxwell, 2008)

Waldman, Adir, *Arbitrating Armed Conflict: Decisions of the Israel-Lebanon Monitoring Group* (Juris Publishing, 2003)

Wang, Faye Fangfei, *Online Dispute Resolution: Technology, Management and Legal Practice from an International Perspective* (Chandos Publishing Oxford Ltd, 2008)

Warne, Jonathan, *International Commercial Dispute Resolution* (Tottel Publishing, 2008)

Waye, Vicki, *A Guide to Arbitration Practice in Australia* (Professional and Continuing Education, 2001)

Weiler, Todd, *NAFTA Investment Law and Arbitration: Past Issues, Current Practice, Future Prospects* (Transnational Publishers, 2004)

Werlauff, Erik, *Civil Procedure in Denmark* (Kluwer Law International, 2002)

Westberg, John A, *International Transactions and Claims Involving Government Parties: Case Law of the Iran-United States Claims Tribunal* (International Law Institute, 1991)

Wheeler, Bridget, *International Arbitration Rules* (LLP Professional Publishing, 2000)

Wiebe, William, *Alternative Dispute Resolution and Commercial Arbitration in the Kingdom of Cambodia* (University of San Francisco, School of Law, 1996)

Wilner, Gabriel M et al, Domke on Commercial Arbitration: The Law and Practice of Commercial Arbitration (Thomson West, loose-leaf)

Wolf, Ronald Charles, *Trade, Aid, and Arbitrate: The Globalization of Western Law* (Ashgate Publishing Ltd, 2004)

Xavier, Grace, *Law and Practice of Arbitration in Malaysia* (Sweet & Maxwell Asia (Malaysia), 2002)

Yesilirmak, Ali, *Provisional Measures in International Commercial Arbitration* (Kluwer Law International, 2005)

Zekos, Georgios I, *International Commercial and Maritime Arbitration* (Routledge Cavendish, 2008)

Zuberbühler, Tobias et al, *Swiss Rules of International Arbitration: Commentary* (Kluwer Law International, 2005)

Züger, Mario, *Arbitration Under Tax Treaties: Improving Legal Protection in International Tax Law* (IBFD Publications, 2001)

J. Legal Articles

5.28 Legal articles, which may be written by practitioners or scholars, often address single issues in great depth. There are far more relevant legal articles in this area of law than there are treatises and monographs.[39] Legal articles can also provide overviews of arbitration in individual states, which can be very helpful when the state in question is not addressed frequently in the literature or when language issues make independent translation of the relevant materials difficult for lawyers from outside the jurisdiction.

---

[39] For reasons of space, it is impossible to list every relevant article on international commercial arbitration. However, researchers can consult Hans Smit et al, The Pechota Bibliography on Arbitration (JurisNet LLC, loose-leaf), should they wish a more comprehensive bibliographic listing of articles in this field.

Legal articles may appear in a variety of locations, including in practitioner or **5.29** scholarly journals; in resources that contain a variety of materials on international commercial arbitration, including arbitral awards and case extracts; and as individual chapters in books on international commercial arbitration. The easiest way to search for legal articles that appear in periodicals is through commercial legal databases including, but not limited to: KluwerArbitration.com, Hein Online Law Journal Law Library, LexisNexis, or Westlaw. These services help lawyers find specific articles, either by permitting full-text searches and/or by providing tables of contents of different journals. The difficulty with these databases is that they do not reflect the entire universe of available documents. Both LexisNexis and Westlaw are heavily geared towards US law journals, although they are beginning to offer an expanded selection of journals from other nations. The KluwerArbitration.com service provides several of the top international journals in the field (which are not currently available on either LexisNexis or Westlaw), but does not have the same depth as LexisNexis and Westlaw do in regards to general law journals and reviews. As a result, many practitioners find it necessary to obtain subscriptions to several different databases and conduct similar searches on each of the databases to avoid missing relevant articles.

Researching legal articles without the benefit of a subscription to a potentially **5.30** expensive electronic database can be difficult. The most straightforward method of searching for relevant articles is through the use of publications such as the Index to Legal Periodicals, the Index to Foreign Legal Periodicals and Current Law Index. These texts index legal periodicals by author and subject. Furthermore, The Pechota Legal Bibliography on Arbitration lists legal articles by subject matter as well as by country. Several free web-based finding tools are also available, although each has its limitations. These resources include:

Ingenta—<http://www.ingenta.com/>[40]

The Library of the Max Planck Institute for Comparative Public Law and International Law—<http://aleph.mpg.de/F?func=file&file_name= find-b&CON_LNG=eng&local_base=vrh01>

The University Law Review Project—<http://www.lawreview.org/>

Working papers and academic presentations can also be useful to the researcher. **5.31** Many of these are available through legal networks such as the Social Science Research Network ('SSRN').[41]

---

[40] Ingenta is primarily aimed at libraries rather than individuals.
[41] The SSRN covers a variety of subjects. The legal network can be found at <http://www.ssrn.com/lsn/index.html>.

5.32 Following are several lists identifying resources that can contain articles on international commercial arbitration. First are law journals and other periodicals that focus on dispute resolution, including international commercial arbitration. These sources will be very useful in helping researchers find relevant articles. Next are specialist journals on international, comparative, and regional law, followed by general journals. There will be articles on international commercial arbitration in both categories of publications, although not with the same frequency as with publications specializing in dispute resolution. Finally, there appears a list of collected works on international arbitration. The articles in these bound volumes may cover a wide variety of topics.

(1) Specialized arbitration and dispute resolution journals and periodicals

5.33 The country of origin for each publication is indicated in parenthesis if it is not clear from the title of the periodical itself.

ADR News & Views (India)

ADRWORLD.COM (US)

American Journal of Comparative Law (US)

American Journal of International Law (US)

The American Review of International Arbitration (US)

The Arbitration and Dispute Resolution Law Journal (UK)

Arbitration & the Law: AAA General Counsel's Annual Report (US)

Arbitration Canada

Arbitration International (UK)

Arbitration Journal (Korea)

Arbitration Journal (US)

Arbitration Law Monthly (UK)

Arbitration News From Korea (Korea)

Arbitration News: The Newsletter of the Irish Branch of the Chartered Institute of Arbitrators

Arbitration: The Journal of the Chartered Institute of Arbitrators (UK)

The Arbitrator (Australia)

The Arbitrator (US)

The Arbitrator & Mediator (Australia)

ASA Bulletin (Switzerland)

Asian Dispute Review (Hong Kong)

Asian International Arbitration Journal (Singapore)

Australasian Dispute Resolution Journal (Australia)

Australian Dispute Resolution Journal (Australia)

Award Service (US)

Bulletin of the Swiss Arbitration Association

Canadian Arbitration and Mediation Journal

Cardozo Journal of Conflict Resolution (US)

Chartered Institute of Arbitrators Newsletter (UK)

Commercial Dispute Resolution Bulletin (Zimbabwe)

Conflict Resolution Quarterly (US)

Croatian Arbitration Yearbook

DIAC Journal (Dubai)

Dispute Resolution International (UK)

Dispute Resolution Journal (formerly The Arbitration Journal) (US)

Dispute Resolution Magazine (US)

Dispute Resolution Times (US)

Emory Journal of International Dispute Resolution (US)

European Arbitration (France)

GCC Commercial Arbitration Bulletin (Bahrain)

ICA Arbitration Quarterly (India)

ICC International Court of Arbitration Bulletin (Paris)

ICSID Review—Foreign Investment Law Journal (US)

In Touch (Belgium)

International Arbitration Law Review (UK)

International Journal of Dispute Resolution/Betriebs-Berater für Wirt-
schaftsmediation & Schiedsgerichtsbarkeit (Germany)

International Litigation Quarterly (US)

JCA Journal (Japan)

JCA Newsletter (Japan)

Journal de Droit International[42] (also known as 'CLUNET') (France)

The Journal of American Arbitration (US)

---

[42] The Journal de Droit International is primarily published in French, but includes some materials and abstracts in English.

Journal of Conflict Resolution (US)

Journal of Dispute Resolution (US)

Journal of International Arbitration (Switzerland)

LCIA Newsletter (UK)

Mealey's International Arbitration Quarterly Law Review (US)

Mealey's International Arbitration Report (US)

Mealey's International Arbitration Review (US)

Mealey's Litigation Report: Reinsurance (US)

Mediterranean and Middle East Arbitration Quarterly (Cyprus)

Model Arbitration Law Quarterly Reports (France)

Ohio State Journal on Dispute Resolution (US)

Pepperdine Dispute Resolution Law Journal (US)

Permanent Court of Arbitration Annual Report (The Netherlands)

Review of Arbitration in Central & Eastern Europe (Croatia)

Stockholm Arbitration Newsletter (Sweden)

Stockholm Arbitration Report (Sweden)

Stockholm International Arbitration Review (Sweden)

The Vindobona Journal of International Commercial Law and Arbitration (Austria)

Wavelength, The Bulletin of the Japan Shipping Exchange

Willamette Journal of International Law and Dispute Resolution (US)

World Arbitration & Mediation Report (The Netherlands)

World Arbitration and Mediation Review (The Netherlands)

World Trade and Arbitration Materials (The Netherlands)

Yearbook Commercial Arbitration (The Netherlands)[43]

Yearbook on Arbitration and Mediation (US)

(2) Specialized journals on international, regional, and comparative law

5.34 The country of origin for each publication is indicated in parenthesis if it is not clear from the title of the periodical itself.

---

[43] The tables of contents for all of the Yearbooks (which were first published in 1976 and are put out by the International Council for Commercial Arbitration ('ICCA')) can be found at <http://www.arbitration-icca.org/publications/yearbook_table_of_contents.html>.

African Journal of International & Comparative Law (UK)

African Yearbook of International Law (The Netherlands)

American Journal of Comparative Law (US)

American Journal of International Law (US)

American University International Law Review (US)

American University Journal of International Law and Policy (US)

Annual Survey of International and Comparative Law (US)

Arizona Journal of International and Comparative Law (US)

Asia Business Law Review (Singapore)

Asia Pacific Law Review (Hong Kong)

Asian American Law Journal (US)

Asian Pacific American Law Journal (US)

Asian-Pacific Law & Policy Journal (US)

Asian Yearbook of International Law (The Netherlands)

Asper Review of International Business and Trade Law (Canada)

Australian International Law Journal

Australian Journal of Asian Law

Australian Year Book of International Law

Austrian Review of International and European Law

Baltic Yearbook of International Law (The Netherlands)

Berkeley Journal of International Law (US)

Berkeley Journal of Middle Eastern & Islamic Law (US)

Boston College International and Comparative Law Review (US)

Boston University International Law Journal (US)

British Year Book of International Law

Brooklyn Journal of International Law (US)

California Western International Law Journal (US)

Canada-United States Law Journal (Canada)

Canadian International Lawyer

Canadian Year Book of International Law

Cardozo Journal of International and Comparative Law (US)

Caribbean Law Review (Barbados)

Case Western Reserve Journal of International Law (US)

The Chicago Journal of International Law (US)

Chicago-Kent Journal of International & Comparative Law (US)

Chinese Journal of International Law (UK)

Chinese Yearbook of International Law and Affairs (Taiwan)

Columbia Journal of Asian Law (US)

Columbia Journal of East European Law (US)

Columbia Journal of European Law (US)

Columbia Journal of Transnational Law (US)

Columbia Journal of World Business (US)

Common Market Law Review (The Netherlands)

Commonwealth Law Bulletin (UK)

The Comparative and International Law Journal of Southern Africa (Republic of South Africa)

Comparative Labor Law and Policy Journal (US)

Comparative Law Yearbook of International Business (UK)

Connecticut Journal of International Law (US)

Cornell International Law Journal (US)

Currents International Trade Law Journal (US)

Denver Journal of International Law and Policy (US)

Dickinson Journal of International Law (US)

Droit et Pratique du Commerce International/International Trade Law and Practice (France)

Duke Journal of Comparative & International Law (US)

East African Law Journal (Kenya)

Emory International Law Review (US)

European Journal of International Law (UK)

European Review of Private Law (The Netherlands)

Florida Journal of International Law (US)

Fordham International Law Journal (US)

George Washington Journal of International Law Review (US)

Georgetown Journal of International Law (US)

Georgia Journal of International and Comparative Law (US)

German Yearbook of International Law

Gonzaga Journal of International Law (US)

Hague Yearbook of International Law (The Netherlands)

Harvard International Law Journal (US)

Hastings International and Comparative Law Review (US)

Hertfordshire Law Journal (UK)

Hofstra Journal of International Business and Law (US)

Houston Journal of International Law (US)

ILSA Journal of International and Comparative Law (US)

ILSA Quarterly (US)

Indian Journal of International Law (India)

Indiana International & Comparative Law Review (US)

Indiana Journal of Global Legal Studies (US)

Inter-American Law Review (US)

The International and Comparative Corporate Law Journal (UK)

International and Comparative Law Quarterly (UK)

International Business Law Journal (UK)

International Business Law Review (formerly Academy of Legal Studies in Business International Business Law Journal) (US)

International Business Lawyer (UK)

International Construction Law Review (UK)

International Encyclopedia of Comparative Law (The Netherlands)

International Insurance Law Review (UK)

International Journal of Baltic Law (Lithuania/US)

The International Journal of Evidence and Proof (UK)

International Journal of Legal Information (US)

International Law FORUM du Droit International (The Netherlands)

International Law Forum of Hebrew University of Jerusalem (Israel)

The International Lawyer (US)

International Sports Law Review (UK)

International Trade Law Journal (US)

International Yearbook of Private Law (Germany/Switzerland)

Irish Yearbook of International Law

Japanese Annual of International Law

Journal of African Law (UK)

Journal of Comparative Law (UK)

Journal of East Asia and International Law (South Korea)

Journal of East European Law (US)

Journal of Eurasian Law (US)

Journal of International Economic Law (UK)

The Journal of International Economic Law (US)

Journal of International Law and International Relations (Canada)

Journal of International Law and Practice (US)

Journal of International Trade Law and Policy (UK)

Journal of Malaysian & Comparative Law (Malaysia)

Journal of Maritime Law and Commerce (US)

Journal of Private International Law (UK)

Journal of South Pacific Law (Vanuatu)

Journal of Transnational Law & Contemporary Problems (US)

Journal of Transnational Law and Policy (US)

Journal of World Investment (Switzerland)

Journal of World Trade Law (UK)

Korean Journal of Comparative Law (South Korea)

Korean Journal of International and Comparative Law (South Korea)

Law and Business Review of the Americas (US)

Law and Practice of International Courts and Tribunals (The Netherlands)

Law & Policy in International Business (US)

Leiden Journal of International Law (The Netherlands)

Lloyd's Maritime and Commercial Law Quarterly (UK)

Lloyd's Maritime Law Newsletter (UK)

London International Law Review (UK)

Loyola of Los Angeles International and Comparative Law Review (US)

Loyola University of Chicago International Law Review (US)

Manchester Journal of International Economic Law (UK)

Maritime Law Journal (US)

Maritime Law Review (Japan)

Maryland Journal of International Law and Trade (US)

Melbourne Journal of International Law (Australia)

Michigan Journal of International Law (US)

Michigan State Journal of International Law (US)

Michigan Yearbook of International Legal Studies (US)

Minnesota Journal of International Law (US)

Netherlands International Law Review (The Netherlands)

Netherlands Yearbook of International Law (The Netherlands)

New England Journal of International and Comparative Law (US)

New York International Law Review (US)

New York Law School Journal of International and Comparative Law (US)

New York University Journal of International Law and Politics (US)

New Zealand Yearbook of International Law

North Carolina Journal of International Law and Commercial Regulation (US)

Non-State Actors and International Law (The Netherlands)

Nordic Journal of International Law (The Netherlands)

North Carolina Journal of International Law and Commercial Regulation (US)

Northwestern Journal of International Law & Business (US)

Oregon Review of International Law (US)

Oxford University Comparative Law Forum (UK)

Pace International Law Review (US)

Pacific Rim Law and Policy Journal (US)

Penn State International Law Review (US)

Polish Yearbook of International Law

Review of Central and East European Law (The Netherlands)

Review of International Business Law (Canada)

San Diego International Law Journal (US)

Santa Clara Journal of International Law (US)

Singapore Year Book of International Law

South African Yearbook of International Law (Republic of South Africa)

South Carolina Journal of International Law and Business (US)

Southwestern Journal of International Law (formerly Southwestern Journal of Law and Trade in the Americas) (US)

Spanish Yearbook of International Law

Sri Lanka Journal of International Law

Stanford Journal of International Law (formerly Stanford Journal of International Studies) (US)

Suffolk Transnational Law Journal (US)

Swiss Review of International Competition Law (Switzerland)

Syracuse Journal of International Law and Commerce (US)

Temple International and Comparative Law Journal (US)

Texas International Law Journal (US)

Tilburg Law Review: Journal of International and Comparative Law (formerly Tilburg Foreign Law Review) (The Netherlands)

Touro International Law Review (US)

Transnational Law and Contemporary Problems (US)

Transnational Lawyer (US)

Tulane Journal of International and Comparative Law (US)

Tulane Maritime Law Journal (US)

Tulsa Journal of Comparative & International Law (US)

UC Davis Journal of International Law & Policy (US)

UCLA Journal of International Law and Foreign Affairs (US)

UCLA Journal of Islamic and Near Eastern Law (US)

UCLA Pacific Basin Law Journal (US)

UNCITRAL Yearbook (Austria)

Uniform Law Review/Revue du Droit Uniforme (Italy)

United States-Mexico Law Review (US)

University of Miami Inter-American Law Review (US)

University of Miami International and Comparative Law Review (formerly University of Miami Yearbook of International Law) (US)

University of Pennsylvania Journal of International Law (formerly University of Pennsylvania Journal of International Economic Law, University of Pennsylvania Journal of International Business Law, and Journal of Comparative Business and Capital Market Law) (US)

Vanderbilt Journal of Transnational Law (US)

Virginia Journal of International Law (US)

Washington University Global Studies Law Review (US)

Wisconsin International Law Journal (US)

Yale Journal of International Law (US)

Yearbook Maritime Law (The Netherlands)

(3) General journals that may carry articles on international commercial arbitration

The country of origin for each publication is indicated in parenthesis if it is not **5.35** clear from the title of the periodical itself.

Adelaide Law Review (Australia)

Akron Law Review (US)

Alabama Law Review (US)

Albany Law Review (US)

Alberta Law Review (Canada)

American Business Law Journal (US)

American Law Review (US)

American University Law Review (US)

Appalachian Journal of Law (US)

Arizona Law Review (US)

Arizona State Law Journal (US)

Arkansas Law Review (US)

Australia Law Journal

Baylor Law Review (US)

Bond Law Review (Australia)

Boston College Law Review (US)

Boston University Law Review (US)

Brigham Young University Law Review (US)

Brooklyn Law Review (US)

Buffalo Law Review (US)

Calcutta Law Journal (India)

California Law Review (US)

California Western Law Review (US)

Cambridge Law Journal (UK)

Canadian Bar Review

Cardozo Law Review (US)

Catholic University Law Review (US)

China Law Review (US)

Cincinnati Law Review (US)

Cleveland State Law Review (US)

Columbia Business Law Review (US)

Columbia Law Review (US)

Commercial Law Journal (US)

Connecticut Law Review (US)

Construction Law Journal (UK)

Cornell Law Review (US)

Creighton Law Review (US)

Cumberland Law Review (US)

Dalhousie Law Journal (Canada)

Delhi Law Review (India)

Denver University Law Review (US)

DePaul Law Review (US)

Drake Law Review (US)

Dublin University Law Journal (Ireland)

Duke Law Journal (US)

Duquesne Law Review (US)

Edinburgh Law Review (UK)

Emory Law Journal (US)

Federal Law Review (Australia)

Florida A&M University Law Review (US)

Florida Coastal Law Review (US)

Florida Law Review (formerly University of Florida Law Review) (US)

Florida State University Law Review (US)

Fordham Law Review (US)

George Mason Law Review (US)

George Washington Law Review (US)

Georgetown Law Journal (US)

Georgia Law Review (US)

Georgia State University Law Review (US)

Golden Gate University Law Review (US)

Gonzaga Law Review (US)

Hamline Law Review (US)

Harvard Law Review (US)

Harvard Negotiation Law Review (US)

Hastings Business Law Journal (US)

Hastings Law Journal (US)

Hofstra Law Review (US)

Hong Kong Law Journal

Houston Law Review (US)

Howard Law Journal (US)

Idaho Law Review (US)

Indian Journal of Legal Studies (India)

Indiana Law Journal (US)

Indiana Law Review (US)

Iowa Law Review (US)

The Irish Jurist (Republic of Ireland)

Israel Law Review (Israel)

John Marshall Law Review (US)

Journal of Business Law (UK)

Journal of Trial Practice & Advocacy (US)

Kansas Law Review (US)

Kentucky Law Journal (US)

King's College Law Journal (UK)

Law and Contemporary Problems (US)

The Law Quarterly Review (UK)

Lewis & Clark Law Review (US)

Louisiana Law Review (US)

Loyola Law Review (US)

Loyola of Los Angeles Law Review (US)

Loyola University of Chicago Law Journal (US)

Macquarie Journal of Business Law (Australia)

Maine Law Review (US)

Malayan Law Journal (Malaysia)

Marquette Law Review (US)

Maryland Law Review (US)

McGeorge Law Review (US)

McGill Law Journal (Canada)

Melbourne University Law Review (Australia)

Michigan Law Review (US)

Michigan State Law Review (US)

Minnesota Law Review (US)

Mississippi Law Journal (US)

Missouri Law Review (US)

The Modern Law Review (UK)

Montana Law Review (US)

Nebraska Law Review (US)

Nevada Law Journal (US)

New England Law Review (US)

The New Law Journal (UK)

New Mexico Law Review (US)

New York City Law Review (US)

New York Law Journal (US)

New York Law School Law Review (US)

New York University Law Review (US)

New Zealand Law Journal

New Zealand Law Review

North Carolina Law Review (US)

North Dakota Law Review (US)

Northern Illinois University Law Review (US)

Northern Kentucky Law Review (US)

Northwestern University Law Review (US)

Notre Dame Law Review (US)

Nottingham Law Journal (UK)

Nova Law Review (US)

Ohio Northern University Law Review (US)

Ohio State Law Journal (US)

Oklahoma City University Law Review (US)

Oklahoma Law Review (US)

Oregon Law Review (US)

The Original Law Review (Australia)

Osgood Hall Law Journal (Canada)

Ottawa Law Review (Canada)

Oxford Journal of Legal Studies (UK)

Pace Law Review (US)

Penn State Law Review (US)

Pepperdine Law Review (US)

Queen's Law Review (Canada)

Queensland Law Society Journal (Australia)

Rutgers Law Journal (US)

Rutgers Law Review (US)

Saint Louis University Law Journal (US)

San Diego Law Review (US)

Santa Clara Law Review (US)

Saskatchewan Law Review (Canada)

Seattle University Law Review (US)

Securities Law Review (US)

Seton Hall Law Review (US)

Singapore Journal of Legal Studies (formerly University of Malaya Law Review and Malaya Law Review)

South African Law Journal (Republic of South Africa)

South Carolina Law Review (US)

South Dakota Law Review (US)

South Texas Law Review (US)

Southern California Law Review (US)

Southern Illinois University Law Journal (US)

Southern Methodist University Law Review (US)

Southwestern University Law Review (US)

St John's Law Review (US)

Stanford Law Review (US)

Suffolk University Law Review (US)

Sydney Law Review (Australia)

Syracuse Law Review (US)

Temple Law Review (US)

Tennessee Law Review (US)

Texas Law Review (US)

Texas Tech Law Review (US)

Thurgood Marshall Law Review (US)

Touro Law Review (US)

Tulane Law Review (US)

Tulsa Law Review (US)

UCLA Law Review (US)

UMKC Law Review (US)

University of Arkansas at Little Rock Law Review (US)

University of Baltimore Law Review (US)

University of British Columbia Law Review (Canada)

University of Chicago Law Review (US)

University of Cincinnati Law Review (US)

University of Colorado Law Review (US)

University of Dayton Law Review (US)

University of Detroit Law Review (US)

University of Ghana Law Journal

University of Hawai'i Law Review (US)

University of Illinois Law Review (US)

University of Kansas Law Review (US)

University of Miami Law Review (US)

University of Minnesota Law Review (US)

University of New Brunswick Law Journal (Canada)

University of Pennsylvania Law Review (US)

University of Pittsburgh Law Review (US)

University of Queensland Law Journal (Australia)

University of Richmond Law Review (US)

University of San Francisco Law Review (US)

University of Toledo Law Review (US)

University of Toronto Law Journal (Canada)

Utah Law Review (US)

Valparaiso University Law Review (US)

Vanderbilt Law Review (US)

Vermont Law Review (US)

Victoria University of Wellington Law Review (New Zealand)

Villanova Law Review (US)

Virginia Law Review (US)

Wake Forest Law Review (US)

Washburn Law Journal (US)

Washington and Lee Law Review (US)

Washington Law Review (US)

Washington University Law Review (formerly Washington University Law Quarterly) (US)

Wayne Law Review (US)

West Virginia Law Review (US)

Western New England Law Review (US)

Whittier Law Review (US)

William & Mary Law Review (US)

William Mitchell Law Review (US)

Willamette Law Review (US)

Windsor Review of Legal and Social Issues (Canada)

Wisconsin Law Review (US)

Wyoming Law Review (US)

Yale Law Journal (US)

(4) Scholarly and practitioner collections

The following list includes volumes that were compiled by institutional editors.   **5.36**

Aicher, Josef et al (eds), *Decisions of the Arbitral Panel for In Rem Restitution* (Hart Publishing, 2008)

Alvarez, Guillermo Aguilar and W Michael Reisman (eds), *The Reasons Requirement in International Investment Arbitration: Critical Case Studies* (Martinus Nijhoff Publishers, 2008)

Asken, Gerald et al (eds), *Global Reflections on International Law, Commerce and Dispute Resolution: Liber Amicorum in Honour of Robert Briner* (ICC Publications, 2005)

Barin, Babak (ed), *Carswell's Handbook of International Dispute Resolution Rules* (Carswell Legal Publications, 1999)

Beaumont, Ben (ed), Arbitration Procedure in Asia (Sweet & Maxwell Asia, loose-leaf)

Belgian Centre for Arbitration and Mediation (ed), *Arbitration and European Law* (Bruylant, 1997)

Beresford-Hartwell, Geoffrey M (ed), *The Commercial Way to Justice* (Kluwer Law International, 1997)

Berkeley, Andrew and Jacqueline Mimms (eds), *International Commercial Arbitration: Practical Perspectives* (Centre of Construction Law and Management, 2001)

Berti, Stephen V et al (eds), *International Arbitration in Switzerland: An Introduction to and a Commentary on Articles 176–194 of the Swiss Private International Law Statute* (Kluwer Law International, 2000)

Bishop, R Doak (ed), *The Art of Advocacy in International Arbitration* (Juris Publishing, 2004)

Bishop, R Doak et al (eds), *Foreign Investment Disputes: Cases, Materials, and Commentary* (Kluwer Law International, 2005)

Blackaby, Nigel et al (eds), *International Arbitration in Latin American* (Kluwer Law International, 2003)

Blackshaw, Ian S et al (eds), *The Court of Arbitration for Sport* (Cambridge University Press, 2006)

Blanke, Gordon (ed), *Arbitrating Competition Law Issues: A European and a US Perspective* (Kluwer Law International, 2008)

Blessing, Marc (ed), *Investing in Eastern European Countries—and Arbitration: A Collection of Reports and Materials Delivered at the ASA Conference held in Zurich on 11 December 1992* (Swiss Arbitration Association, 1993)

Böckstiegel, Karl-Heinz (ed), *Acts of State and Arbitration* (Carl Heymanns Verlag, 1997)

Bösch, Axel and Joanna Farnsworth (eds), *Provisional Remedies in International Commercial Arbitration: A Practitioner Handbook* (De Gruyter, 1994)

Brand, Ronald A et al (eds), *The Draft UNCITRAL Digest and Beyond* (Sweet & Maxwell, 2003)

Bratspies, Rebecca M and Russell A Miller (eds), *Transborder Harm in International Law: Lessons from the Trail Smelter Arbitration* (Cambridge University Press, 2006)

Briner, Robert et al (eds), *Law of International Business and Dispute Settlement in the 21st Century: Liber Amicorum Karl-Heinz Böckstiegel* (Carl Heymanns Verlag, 2001)

Campbell, Dennis (ed), *Comparative Law Yearbook of International Business: Serving Process and Obtaining Evidence Abroad* (Kluwer Law International, 1998)

Campbell, Dennis (ed), *Dispute Resolution Methods* (Kluwer Law International, 1996)

Campbell, Dennis and Susan Meek (eds), *Comparative Law Yearbook of International Business: The Arbitration Process—Special Issue, 2001* (Kluwer Law International, 2002)

Capper, Phillip (ed), *International Arbitration: A Handbook* (Informa Publishing, 2004)

Carbonneau, Thomas E (ed), *Lex Mercatoria and Arbitration: A Discussion of the New Law Merchant* (JurisNet LLC, 1998)

Carbonneau, Thomas E (ed), *Resolving Transnational Disputes Through International Arbitration* (University of Virginia Press, 1988)

Carbonneau, Thomas E and Jeannette A Jaeggi (eds), *AAA Handbook on Commercial Arbitration* (Juris Publishing, 2006)

Carbonneau, Thomas E and Jeannette A Jaeggi (eds), *AAA Handbook on International Arbitration and ADR* (Juris Publishing, 2006)

Carbonneau, Thomas E and Philip J McConnaughay (eds), *AAA Handbook on Construction Arbitration and ADR* (Juris Publishing, 2007)

Carbonneau, Thomas E and Philip J McConnaughay (eds), *AAA Handbook on Employment Arbitration and ADR* (Juris Publishing, 2007)

Carbonneau, Thomas E and Philip J McConnaughay (eds), *AAA Handbook on Labor Arbitration* (Juris Publishing, 2007)

Carbonneau, Thomas E and Vratislav Pechota (eds), *IUS Arbitrale International: Essays in Honour of Hans Smit* (Juris Publishing, 1993)

Caron, David D and John R Crook (eds), *The Iran-United States Claims Tribunal and the Process of International Claims Resolution: A Study* (Brill Academic Publishers Inc, 2000)

Castro, Leonel Pereznieto et al (eds), *Tradition and Innovation in Private International Law at the Beginning of the Third Millennium* (Juris Publishing, 2006)

CEPANI (ed), *Arbitral Procedure at the Dawn of the New Millennium* (Bruylant, 2004)

Clark, Roger S et al (eds), *International and National Law in Russia and Eastern Europe: Essays in Honor of George Ginsburgs* (Martinus Nijhoff Publishers, 2001)

Cohen, Jerome A et al (eds), *Arbitration in China: A Practical Guide* (Sweet & Maxwell Asia, 2007)

Coleman, Anthony (ed), Encyclopedia of International Commercial Litigation (Kluwer Law International, loose-leaf)

Cranston, Ross (ed), *Making Commercial Law; Essays in Honour of Roy Goode* (Oxford University Press, 1997)

Cremades, Bernardo M and Julian DM Lew (eds), *Parallel State and Arbitral Procedures in International Arbitration* (Kluwer Law International, 2006)

Davies, Edward et al (eds), *Dispute Resolution and Conflict Management in Construction: An International Perspective* (Taylor and Francis, 1998)

Davis, Benjamin G (ed), *Improving International Arbitration: The Need for Speed and Trust: Liber Amicorum Michel Gaudet* (ICC Publishing, 1998)

de Palo, Guiseppe and Mary B Trevor (eds), *Arbitration and Mediation in the Southern Mediterranean Countries* (Kluwer Law International, 2007)

Derains, Yves, and Richard H Kreindler (eds), *Evaluation of Damages in International Arbitration* (ICC Publishing, 2006)

de Zylva, Martin Odams and Reziya Harrison (eds), *International Commercial Arbitration for the New Millennium* (Jordans Ltd, 2000)

Diaz, Luis Miguel and Nancy A Oretskin (eds), *Commercial Mediation & Arbitration in the NAFTA Countries* (Juris Publishing, 1999)

Dickinson, Andrew et al (eds), *Butterworths International Commercial Litigation Handbook* (LexisNexis Butterworths, 2006)

Drahozal, Christopher R and Richard W Naimark (eds), *Towards a Science of International Arbitration: Collected Empirical Research* (Kluwer Law International, 2005)

Eijsvoogel, Peter V (ed), *Evidence in International Arbitration Proceedings* (Kluwer Law International, 2001)

Einhorn, Talia and Kurt Siehr (eds), *Intercontinental Cooperation Through Private International Law: Essays in Memory of Peter M Nygh* (Cambridge University Press, 2004)

Fellas, John (ed), Transnational Litigation: A Practitioner's Guide (Oxford University Press, loose-leaf)

Fenn, Pete and Rod Gameson (eds), *Construction Conflict Management and Resolution* (Taylor and Francis, 1992)

Fletcher, Ian F et al (eds), *Foundations and Perspectives on International Trade Law* (Sweet & Maxwell, 2001)

Freeman, Michael (ed), *Alternative Dispute Resolution* (Ashgate Publishing Ltd, 1995)

Frommel, Stefan N and Barry AK Rider (eds), *Conflicting Legal Cultures in Commercial Arbitration: Old Issues and New Trends* (Kluwer Law International, 1999)

Gaillard, Emmanuel (ed), *Transnational Rules in International Commercial Arbitration* (ICC Publishing, 1993)

Gaillard, Emmanuel et al (eds), *Anti-Suit Injunctions in International Arbitration* (Juris Publishing, 2005)

Gaillard, Emmanuel and Yas Banifatemi (eds), *Annulment of ICSID Awards* (Juris Publishing, 2004)

Gaillard, Emmanuel and Yas Banifatemi (eds), *Precedent in International Arbitration* (Juris Publishing, 2008)

Gaillard, Emmanuel and John Savage (eds), *Fouchard, Gaillard, Goldman on International Commercial Arbitration* (Kluwer Law International, 1999)

Gaillard, Emmanuel and Jennifer Youman (eds), *State Entities in International Arbitration* (Juris Publishing, 2008)

Garnett, Richard et al (eds), *A Practical Guide to International Commercial Arbitration* (Oceana Publications, 2000)

Garro, Alejandro M (ed), *Commercial and Labor Arbitration in Central America* (Transnational Juris Pub, 1991)

Gibson, Christopher S and Christopher R Drahozal (eds), *The Iran-U.S. Claims Tribunal at 25: The Cases Everyone Needs to Know for Investor-State and International Arbitration* (Oxford University Press, 2007)

Goldscheider, Robert and Michael De Haas (eds), Arbitration and the Licensing Process (Clark Boardman Callaghan, loose-leaf)

Goldsmith, Jack L (ed), *International Dispute Resolution: The Regulation of Forum Selection: Fourteenth Sokol Colloquium* (Martinus Nijhoff Publishers, 1997)

Goldsmith, Jean-Claude et al (eds), *ADR in Business: Practice and Issues Across Countries and Cultures* (Kluwer Law International, 2005)

Hamilton, P et al (eds), *The Permanent Court of Arbitration: International Arbitration and Dispute Resolution—Summaries of Awards, Settlement Agreements and Reports* (Kluwer Law International, 1999)

Hascher, Dominique (ed), *Collection of Procedural Decisions in ICC Arbitration* (Kluwer Law Publishing, 1997)

Helgeson, Edward and Elihu Lauterpacht (eds), *Reports of Cases Decided under the Convention on the Settlement of Investment Disputes between States and Nationals of Other States 1965* (Cambridge University Press, 2002)

Heuman, Lars and Sigvard Jarvin (eds), *The Swedish Arbitration Act of 1999, Five Years On: A Critical Review of Strengths and Weaknesses* (Juris Publishing, 2006)

Holtzmann, Howard M and Edda Kristjánsdóttir (eds), *International Mass Claims Processes: Legal and Practical Perspectives* (Oxford University Press, 2007)

Honsell, Heinrich et al (eds), *International Arbitration in Switzerland* (Kluwer Law International, 2000)

Horn, Ben and Roger Hopkins (eds), *Arbitration Law Handbook* (Informa Publishing, 2007)

Horn, Norbert and Stefan Kröll (eds), *Arbitrating Foreign Investment Disputes: Procedural and Substantive Legal Aspects* (Kluwer Law International, 2004)

Horn, Norbert and Joseph J Norton (ed), *Nonjudicial Dispute Settlement in International Financial Transactions* (Kluwer Law International, 2000)

Howell, David J (ed), *Electronic Disclosure in International Arbitration* (Juris Publishing, 2009)

Hunter, Martin et al (eds), *Internationalization of International Arbitration* (Kluwer Law International, 1995)

International Bar Association (ed), *Enforcement of Arbitration Agreements in Latin America: Papers Presented at the 1998 Vancouver IBA Conference* (Kluwer Law International, 1999)

International Bureau of the Permanent Court of Arbitration (ed), *Permanent Court of Arbitration Centennial Papers: International Alternative Dispute Resolution—Past, Present and Future* (Kluwer Law International, 2000)

International Centre for Settlement of Investment Disputes (ed), Investment Laws of the World (Oxford University Press, loose-leaf)

International Centre for Settlement of Investment Disputes (ed), Investment Promotion and Protection Treaties (Oxford University Press, loose-leaf)

International Council for Commercial Arbitration ('ICCA'), Congress Series (Kluwer Law International, loose-leaf)[44]

---

[44] The tables of contents for the various ICCA Congress publications—which have come out intermittently since 1982—can be found at <http://www.arbitration-icca.org/publications/

International Fiscal Association, *Resolution of Tax Treaty Conflicts by Arbitration* (Kluwer Law International, 1994)

Jarvin, Sigvard and Annette Magnusson (eds), *International Arbitration Court Decisions* (Juris Net LLC, 2008)

Jarvin, Sigvard and Annette Magnusson (eds), *SCC Arbitral Awards 1999– 2003* (Juris Publishing, 2006)

Juenger, Frederich K (ed), *Choice of Law and Multistate Justice* (Transnational Publishers, 2005)

Karrer, Pierre A (ed), *Arbitral Tribunals or State Courts: Who Must Defer to Whom? ASA Special Series No 15* (Swiss Arbitration Association, 2001)

Karrer, Pierre A (ed), *The Claims Resolution Process on Dormant Accounts in Switzerland, ASA Special Series No 13, 2000* (Swiss Arbitration Association, 2000)

Karrer, Pierre A (ed), *Dispute Resolution on International Markets: International Arbitration—Do's and Don'ts, ASA Special Series No 25, 2005* (Swiss Arbitration Association, 2005)

Karsten, Kristine and Andrew Berkeley (eds), *Arbitration: Money Laundering, Corruption, and Fraud* (Kluwer Law International, 2003)

Kaufmann-Kohler, Gabrielle and Thomas Schultz (eds), *Online Dispute Resolution: Challenges for Contemporary Justice* (Kluwer Law International, 2004)

Kaufmann-Kohler, Gabrielle and Blaise Stucki (eds), *International Arbitration in Switzerland: A Handbook for Practitioners* (Kluwer Law International, 2004)

Kaufmann-Kohler, Gabrielle and Blaise Stucki (eds), *The Swiss Rules of International Arbitration* (Swiss Arbitration Association, 2004)

Kemicha, Fathi (ed), *Euro-Arab Arbitration I* (Lloyd's of London Press, 1987)

Kemicha, Fathi (ed), *Euro-Arab Arbitration II* (Graham & Trotman, 1989)

Kemicha, Fathi (ed), *Euro-Arab Arbitration III* (Graham & Trotman, 1990)

Legum, Barton (ed), *International Litigation Strategies and Practice* (American Bar Association, 2005)

Levy, Laurent and VV Veeder (eds), *Arbitration and Oral Evidence* (Kluwer Law International, 2006)

---

congress_series_table_of_contents.html>. The series were edited first by Pieter Sanders then by Albert Jan van den Berg, and are listed in this section individually under those editors' names.

Lew, Julian DM (ed), *Contemporary Problems in International Arbitration* (Kluwer Academic Publishers, 1987)

Lew, Julian DM (ed), *Immunity of Arbitrators* (LLP Ltd, 1990)

Lew, Julian DM and Loukas A Mistelis (eds), *Arbitration Insights: Twenty Years of the Annual Lecture of the School of International Arbitration* (Kluwer Law International, 2006)

Liebscher, Christoph and Alice Fremuth-Wolf (eds), *Arbitration Law and Practice in Central and Eastern Europe* (Juris Publishing, 2006)

Lillich, Richard B (ed), *Fact-Finding Before International Tribunals* (Transnational Publishers, 1991)

Lillich, Richard B (ed), *The Iran-United States Claims Tribunal 1981–83* (The University Press of Virginia, 1984)

Lillich, Richard B et al (eds), *The Iran-United States Claims Tribunal: Its Contribution to the Law of State Responsibility* (Transnational Publishers, 1998)

Lillich, Richard B and Charles Brower (eds), *International Arbitration in the 21st Century: Towards Judicialization and Uniformity?* (Transnational Publishers, 1994)

Lowenfeld, Andreas and Linda J Silberman (eds), *The Hague Convention on Jurisdiction and Judgments* (Juris Publishing, 2001)

Mackie, Karl J (ed), *A Handbook of Dispute Resolution* (Routledge, 1991)

McConnaughay, Philip J and Thomas B Ginsburg (eds), *International Commercial Arbitration in Asia* (Juris Publishing, 2006)

Mealey's Special Report: Enforcement of ICC Awards in International Arbitration (LexisNexis, 2001)

Medalie, Richard J (ed), *Commercial Arbitration for the 1990s* (American Bar Association, 1991)

Mei-Fung, Pricilla Leung (ed), *Selected Works of China International Economic and Trade Arbitration Commission* (Sweet & Maxwell, 1996)

Mei-Fung, Pricilla Leung (ed), *Selected Works of China Maritime Commission* (XPL Law, 2004)

Min, Eun-Joo and Matthias Lilleengen (eds), *Collection of WIPO Domain Name Panel Decisions* (Kluwer Law International, 2004)

Mistelis, Loukas A and Julian DM Lew (eds), *Pervasive Problems in International Arbitration* (Kluwer Law International, 2006)

Moffitt, Michael L and Robert C Bordone (eds), *The Handbook of Dispute Resolution* (Jossey Bass, 2005)

Moser, Michael J (ed), Arbitration in Asia (Juris Publishing, loose-leaf)

Moser, Michael J (ed), *Business Disputes in China* (Juris Publishing, 2007)

Moser, Michael J (ed), *Investor-State Arbitration: Lessons for Asia* (Juris Publishing, 2008)

Mourra, Mary Helen et al (eds), The Pechota Bibliography on Arbitration (Juris Publishing, loose-leaf)

Muller, Sam and Wim Mijs (eds), *The Flame Rekindled: New Hopes for International Arbitration* (Martinus Nijhoff Publishers, 1994)

Newman, Lawrence W (ed), Securing & Enforcing Judgments in Latin America (Juris Publishing, loose-leaf)

Newman, Lawrence W and Grant Hanessian (eds), *International Arbitration Checklists* (Juris Publishing, 2008)

Newman, Lawrence W and Richard D Hill (eds), *The Leading Arbitrators' Guide to International Arbitration* (Juris Publishing, 2008)

Pinsolle, Philipe et al (eds), *Towards A Uniform International Arbitration Law?* (Juris Publishing, 2005)

Pryles, Michael (ed), *Dispute Resolution in Asia* (Kluwer Law International, 2006)

Pryles, Michael and Michael Moskin (eds), *The Asian Leading Arbitrators' Guide to International Arbitration* (Juris Publishing, 2007)

Ribeiro, Clarisse (ed), *Investment Arbitration and the Energy Charter Treaty* (Juris Publishing, 2006)

Rose, FD (ed), *International Commercial and Maritime Arbitration* (Sweet & Maxwell, 1988)

Rosenne, Shabtai (ed), *The Hague Peace Conferences of 1899 and 1907 and International Arbitration: Reports and Documents* (TMC Asser Press, 2001)

Rovine, Arthur W (ed), *Contemporary Issues in International Arbitration and Mediation: The Fordham Papers* (Martinus Nijhoff Publishers, 2008)

Rowley, J William (ed), *Arbitration World: Jurisdictional Comparison* (The European Lawyer, 2004)

Rubin, Seymour and Dean C Alexander (eds), *NAFTA Law and Policy Series: NAFTA and Investment* (Kluwer Law International, 1995)

Sands, Phillippe et al (eds), *Manual on International Courts and Tribunals* (Butterworths, 1999)

Sanders, Pieter (ed), *Comparative Arbitration Practice and Public Policy in Arbitration* (Kluwer Law International, 1987)

Sanders, Pieter (ed), *ICCA Congress Series No 1, New Trends in the Development of International Commercial Arbitration and the Role of Arbitral and other Institutions* (Kluwer Law International, 1983)

Sanders, Pieter (ed), *ICCA Congress Series No 2, UNCITRAL's Project for a Model Law on International Commercial Arbitration* (Kluwer Law International, 1984)

Sanders, Pieter (ed), *ICCA Congress Series No 3, Comparative Arbitration Practice and Public Policy in Arbitration* (Kluwer Law International, 1987)

Sanders, Pieter (ed), *ICCA Congress Series No 4, Arbitration in Settlement of International Disputes involving the Far East and Arbitration in Combined Transportation* (Kluwer Law International, 1989)

Sarcevic, Petar (ed), *Essays on International Commercial Arbitration* (Graham & Trotman, 1989)

Schäfer, Erik et al (eds), *ICC Arbitration in Practice* (Kluwer Law International, 2004)

Shackleton, Stewart (ed), *Arbitration Law Reports and Review* (Oxford University Press, 2008)[45]

Siekmann, Robert CR and Janwilliam Soek (ed), *Arbitral and Disciplinary Rules of International Sports Organisations* (Cambridge University Press, 2001)

Singapore International Arbitration Centre (ed), *The Cedric Barclay Lectures* (Singapore International Arbitration Centre, 2006)

Singapore International Arbitration Centre (ed), *Celebrating Success: 20 Years, UNCITRAL Model Law on International Commercial Arbitration* (Singapore International Arbitration Centre, 2006)

Singapore International Arbitration Centre (ed), *Celebrating Success: 25 Years, United Nations Convention on Contracts for the International Sale of Goods* (Singapore International Arbitration Centre, 2006)

Singapore International Arbitration Centre (ed), *ICMA XVI Congress Papers Singapore* (Singapore International Arbitration Centre, 2007)

Singapore International Arbitration Centre (ed), *Institutional Arbitration in Asia* (Singapore International Arbitration Centre, 2005)

Smit, Hans (ed), *WIPO Arbitration Rules: Commentary and Analysis* (Juris Publishing, 2000)

Smit, Hans and Vratislav Pechota (eds), *International Commercial Arbitration and the Courts* (Juris Publishing, 2004)

---

[45] This is a series of six annual volumes covering the years 2000 to 2005.

Smit, Hans and Vratislav Pechota (eds), The Roster of International Arbitrators (Juris Publishing, loose-leaf)

Soons, AHA (ed), *International Arbitration: Past and Prospects* (Martinus Nijhoff Publishers, 1990)

St Antoine, Theodore J (ed), *The Common Law of the Workplace: The Views of Arbitrators* (BNA Books, 2005)

Stockholm Chamber of Commerce (ed), Arbitration in Sweden: Yearbook of the Arbitration Institute of the Stockholm Chamber of Commerce (Juris Publishing, annual)[46]

Sumampouw, Mathilde et al (eds), *Law and Reality: Essays on National and International Procedural Law in Honour of Cornelis Carel Albert Voskuil* (Martinus Nijhoff Publishers, 1992)

Swiss Arbitration Association (ed), *Arbitration in Banking and Financial Matters* (Swiss Arbitration Association, 2003)

Swiss Arbitration Association (ed), *Arbitration of Merger and Acquisition Disputes* (Swiss Arbitration Association, 2005)

Swiss Arbitration Association (ed), *Arbitration of Sports-Related Disputes* (Swiss Arbitration Association, 1998)

Swiss Arbitration Association (ed), *Best Practices in International Arbitration* (Swiss Arbitration Association, 2006)

Swiss Arbitration Association (ed), *Conflicts of Interest in International Commercial Arbitration* (Swiss Arbitration Association, 1998)

Swiss Arbitration Association (ed), *Investment Treaties and Arbitration* (Swiss Arbitration Association, 2002)

Swiss Arbitration Association (ed), *Objective Arbitrability—Antitrust Disputes—Intellectual Property Disputes: A Collection of Reports and Materials Delivered at the ASA Conference Held in Zurich on 19 November 1993* (Swiss Arbitration Association, 1994)

Swiss Arbitration Association (ed), *The New Swiss Law on International Arbitration* (Swiss Arbitration Association, 1990)

Swiss Arbitration Association (ed), *The New York Convention 1958* (Swiss Arbitration Association, 1996)

Swiss Arbitration Association (ed), *The Swiss Rules of International Arbitration* (Swiss Arbitration Association, 2004)

---

[46] There are three titles in this series, covering the years 1995, 1996, and 1997.

Tackaberry, John A (ed), *International Commercial Arbitration for Today and Tomorrow: A View of Arbitration in the Nineties and Beyond* (Lewes, 1991)

Taniguchi, Yasuhei et al (eds), Civil Procedure in Japan (Juris Publishing, loose-leaf)

van den Berg, Albert Jan (ed), *ICCA Congress Series No 5, Preventing Delay and Disruption of Arbitration—Effective Proceedings in Construction Cases* (Kluwer Law International, 1991)

van den Berg, Albert Jan (ed), *ICCA Congress Series No 6, International Arbitration in a Changing World* (Kluwer Law International, 1994)

van den Berg, Albert Jan (ed), *ICCA Congress Series No 7, Planning Efficient Arbitration proceedings: The Law Applicable in International Arbitration* (Kluwer Law International, 1996)

van den Berg, Albert Jan (ed), *ICCA Congress Series No 8, International Dispute Resolution: Towards an International Arbitration Culture* (Kluwer Law International, 1998)

van den Berg, Albert Jan (ed), *ICCA Congress Series No 9, Improving the Efficiency of Arbitration and Awards: 40 Years of Application of the New York Convention* (Kluwer Law International, 1999)

van den Berg, Albert Jan (ed), *ICCA Congress Series No 10, International Arbitration and the National Courts: The Never Ending Story* (Kluwer Law International, 2001)

van den Berg, Albert Jan (ed), *ICCA Congress Series No 11, International Commercial Arbitration: Important Contemporary Questions* (Kluwer Law International, 2003)

van den Berg, Albert Jan (ed), *ICCA Congress Series No 12, New Horizons for International Commercial Arbitration and Beyond* (Kluwer Law International, 2005)

van den Berg, Albert Jan (ed), *ICCA Congress Series No 13, International Arbitration: Back to Basics?* (Kluwer Law International, 2008)

van den Berg, Albert Jan (ed), *Improving the Efficiency of Arbitration Agreements and Awards* (Kluwer Law International, 1999)

van den Berg, Albert Jan (ed), *International Arbitration in a Changing World* (Kluwer Law International, 1994)

van Rhee, CH and Alan Uzelac (eds), *Public and Private Justice: Dispute Resolution in Modern Societies* (Hart Publishing, 2007)

von Kann, Curtis E et al (eds), *The College of Commercial Arbitrators Guide to Best Practices in Commercial Arbitration* (Juris Publishing, 2006) von Thülen Rhoades, Rufus et al (eds), *Practitioner's Handbook on International Arbitration and Mediation* (Juris Publishing, 2007)

Walker, Janet (ed), *The Vis Book—A Participant's Guide to the Willem C Vis International Commercial Arbitration Moot* (Juris Publishing, 2008)

Weigand, Frank-Bernd (ed), *Practitioner's Handbook on International Arbitration* (CH Beck, 2002)

Weiler, TJ Grierson (ed), *International Investment Law and Arbitration: Leading Cases from the ICSID, NAFTA, Bilateral Treaties and Customary International Law* (Cameron May Ltd, 2005)

Weiler, TJ Grierson (ed), *Investment Treaty Arbitration and International Law* (Juris Publishing, 2008)

Yang, Guohua et al (eds), *WTO Dispute Settlement Understanding: A Detailed Interpretation* (Kluwer Law International, 2005)

Yelpaala, Koyo et al (eds), *Drafting and Enforcing Contracts in Civil and Common Law Jurisdictions* (Springer, 1986)

Zuberbühler, Tobias et al (eds), *Swiss Rules of International Arbitration: Commentary* (Kluwer Law International, 2005)

INDEX